Tough Guy Wisdom

I0170808

Alain Burrese

TGW BOOKS
Missoula, Montana

Also by Alain Burrese:

Books:

Tough Guy Wisdom II: Return of the Tough Guy
Tough Guy Wisdom III: Revenge of the Tough Guy
Lost Conscience
Hard-Won Wisdom From The School Of Hard Knocks

DVDs:

Hapkido Hoshinsul
Streetfighting Essentials
Hapkido Cane
Lock On: Joint Locking Essentials vols. 1-5

Copyright © 2011 Alain Burrese
Print ISBN: 978-1-937872-00-7
eBook ISBN: 978-1-937872-01-4

Published by TGW Books, a division of
Burrese Enterprises, Inc.
Missoula, MT 59801, USA

Cover design by Bryan Whitney.

Neither the author nor the publisher assumes any responsibility for
the use or misuse of information contained in this book.

Visit the Tough Guy Wisdom website: www.toughguywisdom.com

DEDICATION

The *Tough Guy Wisdom* series is dedicated to my wife, Yi-saeng, and our daughter, Cosette. If nothing else, I want to be their "Tough Guy."

INTRODUCTION

I grew up watching tough guy movies, and I have to admit, they are still my favorite genre. Of course I watch other movies, but my favorites are watching a tough guy kicking ass and taking names, righting wrongs, punishing those who deserve it, and most of all – saying the lines the mark the epitome of cool, those lines we remember, repeat, and identify with "Tough Guys."

I'd even repeat the lines for real once in a while when younger and frequenting various watering holes and doing my best to be a tough guy. After all, as an Army paratrooper and sniper, I had to live up to those tough guy role models from the silver screen. I even made up my own tough guy line that I used in a bar or two, "You ain't big enough, and you don't have enough friends." Yeah, I thought I was cool, just like my movie heroes.

I'll also admit, it was Rambo in *First Blood* that influenced me to join the Army, go the Airborne and sniper route, and almost re-up to put in a Special Forces packet. I got out instead, and was influenced by Martin Riggs in the first two *Lethal Weapon* movies to head to Los Angeles and apply for the LAPD. (Yes, one could say I let movies influence me too much.) After being in LA for a bit, making the hiring list, and then speaking with an Army buddy's dad who was a Los Angeles fireman, I decided that going to college was a better choice and decided against wearing the Blue in LA.

The *Billy Jack* movies influenced my interest in the martial art of Hapkido. Many people remember this line from *Billy Jack*, "I'm going to take this right foot, and I'm going to wop you on that side of your face. And you want to know something, there's not a damn thing you're going to be able to do about it." At the time, I never knew I'd eventually live and train in South Korea, teach, write about, and do DVDs on Hapkido, and have the opportunity to train with Grand Master Bong Soo Han, the Korean Hapkido master who performed the actual kick after that famous line. That was definitely a tough guy movie that influenced me in a very positive way.

Now, a bit older and a bit wiser, I don't go out looking for opportunities to use tough guy lines and get in trouble as I used to, but I still enjoy watching tough guy movies, both new ones that come out, and revisiting those of yesteryear that I grew up with. That's why working on the *Tough Guy Wisdom* series has been a lot of fun. I watched every movie to collect the quotes for these books and information for this series. I also used on-line and print sources to find the movie and actor trivia that the books contain. The Internet Movie Database, IMDb, provided much assistance in writing these books, as did other sources. I'm grateful to them all.

Some quotes, such as "I'm the best." (Found in this volume.) don't seem "tough guy," until you have the setting. That's why I included the setting for each quote included in the *Tough Guy Wisdom* series. You need to picture a scared flight attendant saying to Wesley Snipes as John Cutter, "Tell me you're good at this" in regards to Cutter dealing with the terrorists on the plane. This was Cutter's response in *Passenger 57* (1992). It's the wise-cracking and coolness in the face of danger or difficult situations that helps endear us to these tough guy heroes.

You will notice an absence of a few of the most famous of tough guys, specifically John Wayne, Clint Eastwood, Charles Bronson, Arnold Schwarzenegger, Sylvester Stallone, and Chuck Norris. These six Hollywood tough guys will each have their own specific volumes in the *Tough Guy Wisdom* series. So, if you are a fan of any, or all, of these actors - stay tuned. Collections of their most famous quotes, movie trivia, and facts about them will be appearing in special volumes to be released later.

I wrote this first volume along with volumes two and three, so if you see a couple of quotes from one of your favorite tough guy movies, but wonder why a specific quote is missing, it may be in another volume. Or maybe I missed one that you think should be included. If you have a favorite tough guy movie or quote that you believe should be featured, e-mail me at aburrese@aol.com and it will be considered for a future book in the series.

I sincerely hope that you enjoy reading these tough guy quotes, along with the movie and actor trivia, as much as I enjoyed collecting them. It's pretty cool when you can tell your wife and friends that watching a tough guy movie is actually work. I'm also sure that reading this book will remind you of movies you saw a long time ago and will want to watch again. Take it from me, it is fun to watch them again and remember the first time you saw them, and reminisce a bit. So relax and enjoy a little bit of *Tough Guy Wisdom*.

TOUGH GUY WISDOM

"I think it's time for you gentlemen to leave."

Patrick Swayze as Dalton **– Road House (1989)**

Setting:

Opening line from Dalton when a couple guys are starting trouble in the bar where he is working. The guy stabs Dalton in the arm and wants to fight, but once outside, Dalton walks back in and goes to sew up the cut on his arm.

Movie Trivia:

Road House (1989) was directed by Rowdy Herrington who also directed *Gladiator* (1992) with James Marshall and Cuba Gooding Jr.

About the Actor:

Patrick Swayze played Private Gary Sturgis in an episode of the hit television series *M*A*S*H* (1981).

"Now, I could read you guys your rights, but nah, you guys already know what your rights are don't you. (Three Stooges act) Now that's a real badge, I'm a real cop, and this is a real fucking gun."

Mel Gibson as Sergeant Martin Riggs – **Lethal Weapon (1987)**

Setting:

Martin Riggs confronts four drug dealers in a Christmas tree lot.

Movie Trivia:

This was the first 'action' scene of Riggs after the sniper scene was cut from the movie. Both scenes illustrate that Riggs might be homicidal and someone you don't want to mess with.

About the Actor:

Mel Gibson is a big fan of the Three Stooges.

"Yippee-kai-yay, motherfucker."

Bruce Willis as John McClane – ***Die Hard (1988)***

Setting:

McClane's answer to Hans Gruber's (Alan Rickman) question, "Do you really think you have a chance against us, Mr. Cowboy?"

Movie Trivia:

Die Hard (1988) is based on a 1979 novel by Roderick Thorp titled *Nothing Lasts Forever*, a sequel to the book *The Detective*, which was previously made into a 1968 movie starring Frank Sinatra.

About the Actor:

Walter Bruce Willis was born on March 19, 1955.

"Lady, I never walk into a place I don't know how to walk out of."

Robert De Niro as Sam – **Ronin (1998)**

Setting:

Sam's reply to Deirdre (Natascha McElhone) when she asks what Sam was doing out back, as he retrieves his firearm from where he hid it with the empty bottles outside the back door.

Movie Trivia:

Ronin (1998) was directed by John Frankenheimer, who also directed *French Connection II* (1975), *The Challenge* (1982), *52 Pick Up* (1986), and *Reindeer Games* (2000) among many others.

About the Actor:

Robert De Niro was born on August 17, 1943.

"I don't know who you are. I don't know what you want. If you are looking for ransom, I can tell you I don't have money. But what I do have are a very particular set of skills; skills I have acquired over a very long career. Skills that make me a nightmare for people like you. If you let my daughter go now, that'll be the end of it. I will not look for you, I will not pursue you. But if you don't, I will look for you, I will find you, and I will kill you."

Liam Neeson as Bryan Mills – **Taken (2008, US release 2009)**

Setting:

Mills talks over the phone, and tells Marko (Arben Bajraktaraj), the person who just kidnapped his daughter, what he will do. Marko replies, "good luck." Wrong answer.

Movie Trivia:

Taken (2008, US release 2009) was directed by Pierre Morel, who also directed *From Paris With Love* (2010) starring John Travolta.

About the Actor:

Liam Neeson was born in Northern Ireland, UK.

"All right now…Let's do some good!"

Kevin Costner as Eliot Ness – **The Untouchables (1987)**

Setting:

Ness yells to his men from inside a large truck with snow plow blades on front before crashing through a warehouse's wall where he believes alcohol is being stored. With a reporter there to take pictures, Ness opens a crate to find decorative umbrellas. Later in the movie, two police officers are joking about the incident as one says to the other, "So he gets into the snowplow and he says, 'Let's do some good.' And then, we bust through…" Ness walks in and the laughing and joking cease.

Movie Trivia:

Brian De Palma's first choice to play Al Capone was Robert De Niro, even though the studio hired Bob Hoskins. De Palma insisted on De Niro, and the studio had to pay Hoskins for not using him.

About the Actor:

Kevin Costner was still fairly unknown at the time of casting for *The Untouchables* (1987) and he received the part after some bigger name actors, including Mel Gibson and Harrison Ford, passed on the project.

"Bernard, I want you to know that I try. When Jean and the kids at the school tell me that I'm supposed to control my violent temper and be passive and nonviolent like they are, I try, I really try. But when I see this girl of such a beautiful spirit, so degraded, and when I see this boy that I love sprawled out by this big ape here, and this little girl who is so special to us that we call her God's little gift of sunshine, and I think of the number of years she's going to have to carry in her memory the savagery of this idiotic moment of yours, I just go **BERZERK!**"

Tom Laughlin as Billy Jack – **Billy Jack (1971)**

Setting:

Billy Jack's speech when he goes into the ice cream parlor and finds Bernard Posner (David Roya) and his goons, who had just poured flour over the Native American students who'd gone into the store to buy ice cream. Billy then proceeds to kick butt.

Movie Trivia:

David Roya, who played Bernard Posner, appeared as Derek Johnson in three episodes of *Law & Order* (1999-2003).

About the Actor:

Tom Laughlin played Lt. Buzz Adams in *South Pacific* (1958).

"No. Your advice is good. It's just not good for me."

Tom Selleck as Jesse Stone – ***Stone Cold (2005)***

Setting:

Stone and Abby Taylor (Polly Shannon) discuss his ex-wife and his drinking. This was his reply when she asks, "Are you suggesting that I shut up?"

Movie Trivia:

Robert Harmon directed *Stone Cold* (2005). Harmon also directed *Nowhere To Run* (1993), starring Jean-Claude Van Damme.

About the Actor:

Tom Selleck said about the opening of *Stone Cold* (2005), "It's rather gentle in its place, and yet it gets quite compelling." Selleck said the movie's beginning makes you want to watch it.

"I don't want to shoot you, and you don't want to be dead."

Steven Seagal as Lt. Jack Cole – **The Glimmer Man (1996)**

Setting:

Cole crashes into the school room where Johnny Deverell (Johnny Strong) is holding a bunch of classmates hostage. This is how Cole tries to talk him down. It ends with Cole tackling Johnny through two windows and saying he hated the job.

Movie Trivia:

This line from *The Glimmer Man* (1996) was nearly identical to one from *Silverado* (1985). In that movie, Danny Glover as Malachi 'Mal' Johnson told a group, "Now I don't want to kill you, and you don't want to be dead."

About the Actor:

Steven Seagal has a large gun collection.

"What's the matter ace? Got a little headache?"

Kurt Russell as Gabe Cash – ***Tango & Cash (1989)***

Setting:

After being shot in his bullet proof vest at his apartment, Cash chases down the bad guy and catches up to him when his vehicle crashes. He's sitting there with blood running down his face as Cash leans in the window and asks how he's doing.

Movie Trivia:

During production, the film's title was "The Set Up."

About the Actor:

Kurt Russell was nominated for a 1990 Razzie Award for Worst Supporting Actress for his scene in *Tango & Cash* (1989) where he played in drag.

"From now on, one shot, one kill. No exceptions."

Tom Berenger as Thomas Beckett – ***Sniper (1993)***

Setting:

Beckett chastises Richard Miller (Billy Zane) for firing a warning shot when he was supposed to take out El Cirujano (Ken Radley) on the riverboat.

Movie Trivia:

Several events in the movie were most likely inspired by the life of Carlos Hathcock. Hathcock's story was told by Charles Henderson in the books *Marine Sniper: 93 Confirmed Kills* and *Silent Warrior: The Marine Sniper's Vietnam Story Continues.*

About the Actor:

Tom Berenger was born May 31, 1949, in Chicago, Illinois.

"Hurts, don't it? Now let go of that stud and go on about your business."

Kurt Russell as Wyatt Earp – **Tombstone (1993)**

Setting:

Earp stops a man from whipping a horse and hits him once before telling him to leave.

Movie Trivia:

Tombstone (1993) was written by Kevin Jarre who is also credited for the story *Rambo: First Blood Part II* (1985).

About the Actor:

Kurt Russell's birth name is Kurt Vogel Russell.

"A man's trust is a valuable thing, Button. You don't want to lose it for a handful of cards."

Robert Duval as Boss Spearman – ***Open Range (2003)***

Setting:

Boss passes on some advice to Button (Diego Luna) after catching him cheating at cards when the four are playing to pass time till the rain lets up. Later, Charley Waite (Kevin Costner) continues the lesson by kicking Button off his horse into a stream.

Movie Trivia:

Kevin Costner asked the studio to top-bill Robert Duvall after they originally top-billed Costner over Duvall.

About the Actor:

Robert Selden Duvall was born on January 5, 1931, in San Diego, California.

"Do as I say, and you live."

Samuel L. Jackson as Neville Flynn – **Snakes on a Plane (2006)**

Setting:

The first words Agent Neville Flynn says to Sean Jones (Nathan Phillips) when he saves him from some bad guys out to kill him for witnessing a murder at the beginning of the film.

Movie Trivia:

This line comes back around several times in the movie. Once when Flynn asks Jones if he remembers the first thing he ever said to him, and then at the end when Jones asks Flynn if he remembers the first thing he ever said to him.

About the Actor:

Samuel Leroy Jackson was born on December 21, 1948.

"I think that's quite enough. You are a doctor, after all."

Robert Downey, Jr. as Sherlock Holmes – **Sherlock Holmes (2009)**

Setting:

Sherlock Holmes comments to Dr. John Watson (Jude Law) as Watson applies a sleeper hold to a man that attacked them near the beginning of the movie. Watson lets go of the unconscious man and lets him fall to the ground.

Movie Trivia:

Sherlock Holmes (2009) was nominated for two Oscars: Best Achievement in Art Direction (Sarah Greenwood, art director and Katie Spencer, set decorator); Best Achievement in Music Written for Motion Pictures, Original Score (Hans Zimmer).

About the Actor:

Robert Downey Jr.'s birth name was Robert John Ford-Elias Jr.

"But of course you are dear."

Sean Connery as Capt. John Connor – ***Rising Sun (1993)***

Setting:

Capt. Connor's reply to Eddie Sakamura's (Cary-Hiroyuki Tagawa) bodyguard, Perry (Tony Ganios), when he states as a threat, "You should know I'm a black belt" while trying to prevent Connor and Lt. Webster Smith (Wesley Snipes) from entering the party where Eddie is dancing.

Movie Trivia:

Tony Ganios, who played the black belt bodyguard, Perry, dispatched by the shot to the throat by Sean Connery's character, Capt. John Connor, had a much larger role in the movie *Porky's* (1982) and its sequels *Porky's II: The Next Day* (1983) and *Porky's Revenge* (1985) as Meat Tuperello.

About the Actor:

Thomas Sean Connery was born on August 25, 1930, in Fountainbridge, Edinburgh, Scotland.

"It's a black thing. You wouldn't understand."

Wesley Snipes as John Cutter – ***Passenger 57 (1992)***

Setting:

Cutter's reply to Sly Delvecchio (Tom Sizemore) when Delvecchio asks him, "How do you do that?" in reference to Cutter being hit on by a beautiful security agent when going through the metal detector at the airport security. The movie was made when people without tickets (Sizemore's Delvecchio) could go through security to the boarding gates.

Movie Trivia:

Passenger 57 (1992) was the film debut for Elizabeth Hurley who played Sabrina Ritchie. Prior to this, her screen debut was in *Aria* (1987) and she had been in some television programs.

About the Actor:

According to one on-line biography of Wesley Snipes, he once said, "Lot of the scripts I've been in with other non-white actors haven't been great. Lot of the non-white actors ain't all that great."

"It's already too late."

Vin Diesel as Dominic Toretto – **Fast and Furious (2009)**

Setting:

After Dominic Toretto views the crash site where his former girlfriend Letty (Michelle Rodriquez) was murdered, his sister Mia (Jordana Brewster) pleads with him to let it go, before it's too late. This is what he tells her.

Movie Trivia:

In *Fast and Furious* (2009), the original four actors, Paul Walker, Vin Diesel, Michelle Rodriquez, and Jordana Brewster reunite for this fourth installment of the franchise. All four had not appeared together since the first movie *The Fast and the Furious* (2001).

About the Actor:

Vin Diesel originally wanted to make the 4th and 5th *Fast and Furious* films back to back, but Universal decided to take some time to see how the 4th installment of the franchise would work out before moving on to the 5th.

"A good fight should be like a small play, but played seriously. A good martial artist does not become tense, but ready. Not thinking, yet not dreaming. Ready for whatever may come. When the opponent expands, I contract. When he contracts, I expand. And when there is an opportunity I do not hit. It hits all by itself."

Bruce Lee as Lee – **Enter the Dragon (1973)**

Setting:

Lee discusses philosophy with the elder Abbott (Roy Chiao) of the Shaolin Temple near the beginning of the film.

Movie Trivia:

The opening fight scene is between Bruce Lee and Samo Hung, who went on to become one of Hong Kong's biggest martial arts stars. Samo Hung also starred in 44 episodes of the American television series *Martial Law* (1998-2000), who's character also guest starred on an episode of *Walker, Texas Ranger* (2000) with Chuck Norris.

About the Actor:

Bruce Lee's birth name was Lee Jun Fan. He was born on November 27, 1940, in San Francisco, California.

"Ugly all day."

Nicolas Cage as Cameron Poe – **Con Air (1997)**

Setting:

Poe's reply to Johnny 'Johnny 23' Baca (Danny Trejo), after stopping him from attacking Guard Sally Bishop (Rachel Ticotin), which prompted Johnny 23 to ask, "Do you know what I am?" Johnny 23 then swings on Poe who decks him and says, "This ain't happenin'. Not here, not now."

Movie Trivia:

The three dead cons: Benson, Karls, and Popovich are named after second assistant cameraman Garrett Benson, first assistant cameraman John Karls, and key grip J. Michael Popovich.

About the Actor:

Nicolas Cage, as Nicolas Coppola, played Brad's Bud in the popular teenage comedy *Fast Times at Ridgemont High* (1982).

"I won't be back Pete. I've seen good luck, I've seen bad luck. I know the difference."

Eric Roberts as Merle "The Butcher" Henche – **The Butcher (2007)**

Setting:

Henche is about to leave the table where he just won nineteen thousand dollars, and Chinatown Pete (Bokeem Woodbine) tells him not to come back the next day and to be careful with what he does with the money. This was Henche's reply.

Movie Trivia:

The Butcher (2009) was written and directed by Jesse V. Johnson, who also directed *Pit Fighter* (2005), *The Last Sentinel* (2007), and *Charlie Valentine* (2009) among others.

About the Actor:

Eric Roberts says when he met the director of *The Butcher* (2009), Jesse Johnson, he realized he had to work with him, and if he didn't, he'd be doing himself a disservice because Johnson is the "Coolest."

"You know, I like a man who watches things go on around. It means he'll make his mark someday."

Alan Ladd as Shane – **Shane (1953)**

Setting:

When Shane first rides up and meets Joey (Brandon De Wilde), he says to the boy, "Hello boy. You were watching me down the trail quite a spell, weren't you?" Joey answers, "Yes, I was." Shane tells him the above, and then accepts some water and is startled by Joey cocking his lever action rifle. When Joey says, "Bet you can shoot. Can't ya?" Shane answers, "Little bit."

Movie Trivia:

In 2007, the American Film Institute ranked *Shane* (1953) as the #45 Greatest Movie of All Time.

About the Actor:

Alan Walbridge Ladd was born on September 3, 1913, and died January 29, 1964.

"The difference is, you're still breathing."

Tom Berenger as Jonathan Shale – **The Substitute (1996)**

Setting:

Shale explains the difference between soldiers and killers to Matt Wolfson (Cliff De Young). Shale explains this with his hand squeezing Wolfson's throat. Turns out the cereal Wolfson was eating to keep him regular really worked.

Movie Trivia:

The Substitute (1996) was directed by Robert Mandel.

About the Actor:

Tom Berenger graduated from the University of Missouri, where he majored in journalism.

"Now you get so you can do that with either hand, when you're half-drunk, or half-awake, or inside of a dark room, off the back of a running horse, you might stand a chance. A small chance."

Brian Keith as Jonas Cord – **Nevada Smith (1966)**

Setting:

Cord tells this to the young Max Sand, aka Nevada Smith (Steve McQueen), after shooting a bottle out of the air, just before he starts training Max so he can hunt down those that killed his parents.

Movie Trivia:

Nevada Smith (1966) was based on the part-Indian character from "The Carpetbaggers" by Harold Robbins.

About the Actor:

Brian Keith played many tough guys, but he was also nominated for a Golden Laurel Award for Top Male Comedy Performance in the popular movie *The Parent Trap* (1961).

"It's a funny thing. No matter how low you sink, there's still a right and a wrong. And you always end up choosing. You go one way so you can try to live with yourself. You go the other; you'd still be walking around, but you're dead and you don't know it."

Bruce Willis as John Smith – **Last Man Standing (1996)**

Setting:

Opening narration as John Smith drives down a deserted road…

Movie Trivia:

Last Man Standing (1996) was directed by Walter Hill, who also directed *The Warriors* (1979), *48 Hours* (1982), and *Red Heat* (1988) among others.

About the Actor:

In 1996, the same year *Last Man Standing* (1996) was released, Bruce Willis did the voice of Muddy Grimes in *Beavis and Butt-Head Do America* (1996). Demi Moore, his then wife, was the voice of Dallas Grimes.

"He needed a smack on the head. That's what he got, what's the big deal?"

Tommy Lee Jones as Chief Deputy Marshal Samuel Gerard – *U.S. Marshals (1998)*

Setting:

At a dinner party, Gerard's boss, United States Marshal Catherine Walsh (Kate Nelligan) tells him, "You hit your prisoner while he was in handcuffs. That's against the rules, if he had any brains he'd sue us." Gerard replied, "He bit one of my kids, he got smacked on the head, so what?" She then asks, "Twenty-seven stitches of so what?" Gerard tells her the above.

Movie Trivia:

Stuart Baird directed *U.S. Marshals* (1998).   His other directing credits include *Executive Decision* (1996) and *Star Trek: Nemesis* (2002). He's been the Editor for many more films and has also produced and done other work on a couple of films.

About the Actor:

Tommy Lee Jones won an Oscar for Best Actor in a Supporting Role the first time he portrayed Marshal Sam Gerard in *The Fugitive* (1993).

"The state can flip a switch and kill a man. You can use a gun from a hundred feet away. Or you can poison a man dead and never look him in his eyes. To take a human life with your own two hands is the most soul-crushing thing a man can do. It changes you in a way I can't really explain."

Steve Austin as John Brickner – **Damage (2009)**

Setting:

At the beginning of the movie, Brickner discusses what put him in prison with the parole board. When asked, "Why don't you try?" in regards to being changed, he continues, "You don't just take away a man's life. You carry it with you. It's yours forever. Every action. Every moment. And every thought. It's not something you can shake. Not the best of you anyway."

Movie Trivia:

Damage (2009) was directed by Jeff King, who also directed *Driven to Kill* (2009) and *Kill Switch* (2008), both staring Steven Seagal.

About the Actor:

Steve Austin's autobiography is called *The Stone Cold Truth* by Stone Cold Steve Austin with Jim "J.R." Ross as told to Dennis Brent. It was published in 2003.

"Oh no sir, you ain't seen bad yet. But it's coming."

Patrick Swayze as Truman Gates – **Next of Kin (1989)**

Setting:

Truman Gates confronts John Isabella (Andreas Katsulas) in Isabella's kitchen and asks him to turn over Gates' brother's killer. Isabella says he had nothing to do with it, and says he is sorry for Gates' brother's death and that it is too bad. Gates replies with the above.

Movie Trivia:

Helen Hunt plays Swayze's wife, Jessie Gates, in *Next of Kin* (1989).

About the Actor:

Patrick Swayze teamed up with Larry Gatlin to sing the song "Brothers" for *Next of Kin* (1989).

"Like I told my last wife, I says, 'Honey, I never drive faster than I can see. Besides that, it's all in the reflexes.'"

Kurt Russell as Jack Burton – **Big Trouble in Little China (1986)**

Setting:

Burton, driving his truck at the beginning of the movie, giving out advice over the CB Radio.

Movie Trivia:

Big Trouble in Little China (1986) is one of many tough guy moves that features Jeff Imada doing stunts and in a role. He plays Needles in this film.

About the Actor:

Kurt Russell says he had to learn how to drive a semi truck for his role in *Big Trouble in Little China* (1986), so he could drive the Freightliner owned by character Jack Burton.

"Yeah, well, as far as I'm concerned, progress peaked with frozen pizza."

Bruce Willis as Lt. John McClane – **Die Hard 2 Die Harder (1990)**

Setting:

After being paged, McClane calls his wife, Holly (Bonnie Bedelia) who is still on the plane. He asks if she landed yet, and the above is the reply to her statement, "It's the nineties, remember? Microchips, microwaves, faxes, airphones."

Movie Trivia:

Die Hard 2 Die Harder (1990) was directed by Renny Harlin, who also directed tough guy Sylvester Stallone in *Cliffhanger* (1993) and *Driven* (2001).

About the Actor:

As a youngster, Bruce Willis developed a stutter that posed the threat of social alienation, but he discovered an odd quirk: while performing in front of large numbers of people, the stutter inexplicably vanished.

"Life has a way of making the foreseeable that which never happens, and the unforeseeable that which your life becomes."

Viggo Mortensen as Everett Hitch – ***Appaloosa (2008)***

Setting:

Said in opening monologue as Virgil Cole (Ed Harris) and Everett Hitch ride into Appaloosa where Hitch believes they will be keeping the peace for the foreseeable future.

Movie Trivia:

One of the special features on the DVD is *Historic Accuracy of Appaloosa*, a short piece on how they tried to make everything as historically accurate as possible for the movie.

About the Actor:

Viggo Peter Mortensen, Jr. was born on October 20, 1958, in Manhattan, New York City, New York.

"That's what scares me."

Harrison Ford as Indiana Jones – **Raiders of the Lost Ark (1981)**

Setting:

Upon seeing the golden treasure they are seeking in the opening scene, Indy's guide Satipo (Alfred Molina) tells him, "Let us hurry. There's nothing to fear here." Indy says the above and wisely stops him and discovers the triggers in the floor that launch darts at those who step on them.

Movie Trivia:

Tom Selleck was originally cast as Indiana Jones, but was not able to take the role because he was committed to *Magnum, P.I.* (1980).

About the Actor:

Harrison Ford was born on July 13, 1942.

"Goddamn it, you were right, you know. There wasn't enough room."

Mel Gibson as Sergeant Martin Riggs – **Lethal Weapon 2 (1989)**

Setting:

Riggs' comment to Murtaugh (Danny Glover) after smashing up the side of Murtaugh's wife's car after Murtaugh told him there wasn't enough room to go between the other cars and the guard rail during a high speed chase at the beginning of the movie.

Movie Trivia:

Shane Black, who wrote the first movie, *Lethal Weapon* (1987), worked on the story for this sequel as well, but disagreed with the decision to not kill the character Martin Riggs.

About the Actor:

Mel Gibson's film debut was as an uncredited baseball player in *I Never Promised You a Rose Garden* (1977) starring Kathleen Quinlan.

"You're wearing my hat. What else you got that's mine? I hope your fingers aren't tickling my ivory handled Colt. Stand up real slow and let me see, you might live through the night."

Kevin Kline as Paden – **Silverado (1985)**

Setting:

Paden confronts one of the men who stole his belongings in a saloon.

Movie Trivia:

Silverado's (1995) director, Lawrence Kasdan, offered the role of Jake to Kevin Costner to help make up for Costner's scenes being cut from *The Big Chill* (1983).

About the Actor:

Kevin Kline also stared in Lawrence Kasdan's *The Big Chill* (1983).

"Yeah, you and everybody else."

Kurt Russell as Snake Plissken – **Escape From New York (1981)**

Setting:

Plissken's reply to Brain (Harry Dean Stanton) when the glider goes over the edge of the World Trade Center and they have to opt for another plan. Brain says, "Listen Snake, I swear to God I thought you were dead."

Movie Trivia:

Everyone thought Snake Plissken was dead, just like everyone thought Jacob McCandles (John Wayne) was dead in *Big Jake* (1971).

About the Actor:

Kurt Russell is a card carrying member of the NRA (National Rifle Association).

"That's a slow draw you got there. Sure you want to do that? Shoot a dog in this county on a man's land, I'd bury you in the hill, and tell the sheriff a month or two later. He understands."

Mark Wahlberg as Bob Lee Swagger – **Shooter (2007)**

Setting:

When Colonel Isaac Johnson (Danny Glover) shows up at Swagger's property to recruit him, Johnson's man Jack Payne (Elias Koteas) reaches for his weapon as Swagger readies a blade when discussing Swagger's dog. Johnson diffuses the situation.

Movie Trivia:

Shooter (2007) was based on the Stephen Hunter novel *Point of Impact*, the first of Hunter's Bob Lee Swagger novels.

About the Actor:

Mark Robert Michael Wahlberg was born on June 5th, 1971, in Dorchester, MA.

"Because I'm not going to jail today."

Samuel L. Jackson as Lt. Danny Roman – **The Negotiator (1998)**

Setting:

Roman takes hostages in the city administration building and points a gun at Inspector Terence Niebaum (J.T. Walsh) telling him he wants some answers and they will stay there until Niebaum gives him answers. As they leave Niebaum's office, Roman tells the cops to put their weapons down. When one doesn't, he puts a round into the wall next to the guy's head and says, "That wasn't an accident. And neither will the next one that goes into your head."

Movie Trivia:

The Negotiator (1998) was dedicated in memory of J.T. Walsh who played Terence Niebaum. Walsh died of a heart attack on February 27, 1998, five months before the film was released.

About the Actor:

Samuel L. Jackson married LaTanya Richardson in 1980.

"Let me tell you something. I just got out of prison for something I didn't do, and, before that, I used to, like, you know, study real hard and learned all kinds of different ways to kill motherfuckers just like you."

Steven Seagal as Shane Daniels – ***A Dangerous Man (2009)***

Setting:

After buying a bottle of bourbon, Daniels is confronted by two thugs outside the liquor store. They ask if he wants to buy their car, and then decide to jack him and state he can give them everything he has. This is what he tells them, but they don't listen.

Movie Trivia:

A Dangerous Man (2009) was written and directed by Keoni Waxman who also directed *Hunt to Kill* (2010) with Eric Roberts and Steve Austin.

About the Actor:

Some of the products featured on the official Steven Seagal website are Diamond Lotus Oils, which include: Helichrysum Oil, Juniper Oil, Lavender Oil, Marjram Oil, Melissa Oil, Oregano Oil, Peppermint Oil, and Thyme Oil.

"The truth is a beautiful thing."

Bruce Willis as Joe Hallenbeck – ***The Last Boy Scout (1991)***

Setting:

Hallenbeck suspects his wife Sarah (Chelsea Field) is hiding someone in the closet and tells her she can stop him from shooting through the closet door by telling him the truth. Turns out it's his friend Mike Matthews (Bruce McGill) who was sleeping with his wife. As Matthews tries to explain, Hallenbeck, still holding his gun, says, "It was an accident right? You tripped, slipped on the floor and accidentally stuck your dick in my wife."

Movie Trivia:

The Last Boy Scout (1991) was written by Shane Black and Greg Hicks. Black also wrote *Lethal Weapon* (1987).

About the Actor:

Bruce Willis added twenty pounds to authenticate his physical portrayal of a man whose life has gone to seed in *The Last Boy Scout* (1991).

"You wanna catch Miles? That's fine. I wanna keep Molly alive, and I know what I gotta do. Just stay the hell out of my way."

John Cena as Det. Danny Fisher – *12 Rounds (2009)*

Setting:

Fisher tells Inspector George Aiken (Steve Harris) what he has to do after Aiken tells him, "The fact Miles Jackson (Aidan Gillen) has your girlfriend, mmm, that interests me very little. The fact that he's done something that he never does, the fact that he's shown himself in the city, that interests me quite a bit more."

Movie Trivia:

12 Rounds (2009) was directed by Renny Harlin, who also directed *Cliffhanger* (1993), *The Long Kiss Goodnight* (1996), *Driven* (2001), and *Exorcist: The Beginning* (2004) among many others. This was Harlin's first film to direct with his production company Midnight Sun Pictures.

About the Actor:

John Cena admits to being afraid of heights, and said the stunts involving him rappelling down a building during *12 Rounds* (2009) sucked. He was extremely uncomfortable doing those scenes and said he went home afterwards hating the work and wanting to quit.

"You got clean up on Aisle 4."

Brian Bosworth as Joe Huff/John Stone – **Stone Cold (1991)**

Setting:

At the opening of the movie, suspended police officer Huff takes care of three bad guys robbing a supermarket where he was shopping. Huff's supervisor shows up and asks, "What have you got to say for yourself this time?"

Movie Trivia:

Stone Cold (1991) was directed by Craig R. Baxley, who also directed *Sniper 2* (2002) with Tom Berenger starring as sniper Thomas Beckett.

About the Actor:

The Boz: Confessions of a Modern Anti-Hero is Brian Bosworth's autobiography about his football years, written with Rick Reilly and published in 1988.

"I have long feared that my sins would return to visit me. And the cost is more than I can bear."

Mel Gibson as Benjamin Martin – **The Patriot (2000)**

Setting:

Opening line of the movie as you see a tomahawk and power horn being put into a chest with a knife and other belongings right before the title appears on screen. The line is then said by Martin to Col. Harry Burwell (Chris Cooper) after Martin's son Gabriel Martin (Heath Ledger) is killed.

Movie Trivia:

The Patriot (2000) won two Blockbuster Entertainment Awards. One for Favorite Actor – Drama for Mel Gibson, and the other for Favorite Male – Newcomer for Heath Ledger.

About the Actor:

The Patriot (2000) is one of many films where Mel Gibson portrays a widower. Others include the *Mad Max* series, and the *Lethal Weapon* series.

"I'm telling you straight. It's my way or the highway."

Patrick Swayze as Dalton – **Road House (1989)**

Setting:

Dalton addresses the employees of the Double Deuce after being hired to clean the place up. He gives them a chance to walk if they don't want to follow his rules.

Movie Trivia:

Joel Silver was the Producer of *Road House* (1989), with Executive Producers Tim Moore and Steve Perry. Silver has produced many action films, including the *Lethal Weapon* series, *Commando* (1985), *Exit Wounds* (2001), *Ninja Assassin* (2009), and the *Matrix* series.

About the Actor:

After moving to New York in the 1970s, Patrick Swayze studied different spiritual philosophies, including Buddhist philosophy that really spoke to him.

"I'm one of those boys that appreciates a fine body, regardless of the make."

Vin Diesel as Dominic Toretto – **Fast and Furious (2009)**

Setting:

Toretto's reply to Gisele Harabo's (Gal Gadot) question, "Are you one of those boys who prefers cars to women?" when she finds him in the garage looking at cars.

Movie Trivia:

Fast and Furious (2009) grossed $72.5 million on its opening weekend, the biggest April debut ever and the highest-grossing opening weekend for a car-themed movie.

About the Actor:

Vin Diesel was born on July 18, 1967, in New York, New York.

"Hello. Mr. Sniper, sir! (Shots fired and sniper yells, 'Get away!') I'm still here , asshole! Or do you only do kids?"

Mel Gibson as Sergeant Martin Riggs – **Lethal Weapon (1987)**

Setting:

Martin Riggs confronts a sniper firing out of a window at a school playground and empties his 9mm Beretta into him.

Movie Trivia:

This scene was edited out of the theatrical release and is only seen in the extended director's cut version on DVD.

About the Actor:

Mel Columcille Gerard Gibson was born on January 3, 1956, in Peekskill, New York.

"It's impolite to stick your finger in somebody's chest. Would you like it if I did that to you? All right, hand over the ice pick, please."

Tom Berenger as Jonathan Shale – **The Substitute (1996)**

Setting:

When Shale asks Rodriguez (Vincent Laresca) to hand over an ice pick because he does not allow weapons in class, Rodriguez gets in his face and sticks his finger in Shale's chest. Putting him down with a finger lock, Shale asks for the ice pick again.

Movie Trivia:

Vincent Laresca, who played Rodriguez, appeared in 12 episodes of the popular television hit *24* (2003 – 2004) as Hector Salazar.

About the Actor:

Tom Berenger's second wife was Lisa Berenger. They were married from 1986 to 1997, and had three children: Chelsea (1986), Chloe (1988), and Shiloh Rory (1993).

"Nobody ever told me that before, but I wouldn't go in there."

Robert De Niro as Sam – **Ronin (1998)**

Setting:

Spence (Sean Bean) is about to go into a tunnel to meet the people they are buying weapons from and he wants Sam and Vincent (Jean Reno) to go with him. Sam doesn't want to go into the tunnel and tells Spence, "What are you, crazy?" Spence replies, "You know, you think too hard." The above was Sam's reply.

Movie Trivia:

In an interview regarding *Ronin* (1998), De Niro commented on David Mamet being brought in as a script doctor for the film. Mamet significantly rewrote the script, making major changes to the original by J.D. Zeik. However, after a dispute involving the studio, Mamet used a pseudonym and was credited as Richard Weisz.

About the Actor:

Robert De Niro has gone by several nicknames, including: Bobby Milk (childhood, due to his pallor), Kid Monroe (given to him by Robert Mitchum), Bob, and Bobby D.

"Mister, you ever seen what a Henry rifle can do in the hands of somebody who knows how to use it?"

Danny Glover as Malachi 'Mal' Johnson – ***Silverado (1985)***

Setting:

Mal and his father face off with the cattle hands over the cattle on their farmland.

Movie Trivia:

Lawrence Kasden, director and producer of *Silverado* (1985), cast two of his children and his wife in small roles in the film.

About the Actor:

Danny Lebert Glover was born on July 22, 1946, in San Francisco, California.

"Yeah, I think he better worry."

Mark Wahlberg as Bob Lee Swagger – **Shooter (2007)**

Setting:

Swagger zeros in on a tin can of stew with his sniper rifle and tells his dog, "1,760's a mile. It's a far piece, Sam. Think the President ought to worry?" He then makes the shot and says the above.

Movie Trivia:

Jonathan Lemkin, who wrote the screenplay based on the Stephen Hunter novel *Point of Impact*, was also one of the writers credited with *Lethal Weapon 4* (1998).

About the Actor:

Marky Mark was one of Mark Wahlberg's nicknames. He recorded two albums and toured as Marky Mark and the Funky Bunch.

"A gun is a tool, Marian. No better, no worse than any other tool, an ax, a shovel, or anything. A gun is as good or as bad as the man using it. Remember that."

Alan Ladd as Shane – **Shane (1953)**

Setting:

Marian Starrett (Jean Arthur) interrupts Shane as he's teaching her son, Joey (Brandon De. Wilde), to shoot. She does not want Joey using a gun. Shane shares his philosophy regarding firearms with her.

Movie Trivia:

Brandon De. Wilde was nominated for a 1954 Oscar for Best Actor in a Supporting Role for his performance as Joey Starrett.

About the Actor:

Alan Ladd's first wife was Marjorie 'Midge' Harrold (1936 – 1941) and they had one son, Alan Ladd, Jr.

"It'll hurt if I do."

Bruce Willis as John Smith – **Last Man Standing (1996)**

Setting:

Smith's reply to Finn (Patrick Kilpatrick) after Smith tells Finn he is short on cash and asks if he can help pay the damages. Finn says, "I guess maybe you'll have to kill me," as he opens his coat to reveal his sidearm.

Movie Trivia:

Christopher Walken played Hickey in *Last Man Standing* (1996).

About the Actor:

Bruce Willis played Tony Amato in an episode of *Miami Vice* in 1984.

"Mrs. McCanles, I've got a rifle, a horse, and eight dollars. It'll hold."

Steve McQueen as Max Sand, aka Nevada Smith – **Nevada Smith (1966)**

Setting:

As Max prepares to ride off to search for the three men who killed his mother and father, Mrs. Elvira McCanles (Josephine Hutchinson) tries to give Max money after encouraging him to track them down. This is what he tells her before riding off.

Movie Trivia:

Alan Ladd, most famous for his role as Shane, first portrayed the character Nevada Smith in the movie *The Carpetbaggers* (1964).

About the Actor:

Steve McQueen died November 7, 1980, at the young age of 50 due to cancer.

"Everybody want to be a tough guy, but nobody want to pay the price."

Steven Seagal as Ruslan Drachev – ***Driven To Kill (2009)***

Setting:

In the interrogation room, Detective Norden (Ingrid Torrance) asks Drachev, "You want to be a tough guy?" This is his reply.

Movie Trivia:

Driven To Kill (2009) was directed by Jeff F. King, who also directed Steven Seagal's *Kill Switch* (2008).

About the Actor:

Steven Seagal was one of the Executive Producers for *Driven To Kill* (2009).

"When policemen break the law, then there isn't any law. Just a fight for survival."

Tom Laughlin as Billy Jack – ***Billy Jack (1971)***

Setting:

Billy Jack rides up and stops the slaughter of wild horses at the beginning of the movie. This is his reply to Posner (Bert Freed), who says, "We got the law here Billy Jack."

Movie Trivia:

The theme song to *Billy Jack* (1971) is *One Tin Soldier*, sung by Jinx Dawson of Coven.

About the Actor:

Thomas Robert Laughlin was born in Milwaukee, WI, on August 10, 1931.

"I once talked a man out of blowing up the Sears Tower, but I cannot talk my wife out of a bedroom or my kid off a phone."

Kevin Spacey as Lt. Chris Sabian – **The Negotiator (1998)**

Setting:

Sabian talks to himself in this first scene introducing the character as he tries to negotiate with his wife and daughter while getting ready for a ski trip. Their plans are interrupted when he is called to come and negotiate with hostage taker Danny Roman (Samuel L. Jackson).

Movie Trivia:

The Negotiator (1998) was directed by F. Gary Gray who also directed *The Italian Job* (2003) starring Mark Wahlberg, Charlize Theron, Donald Sutherland, and Jason Statham.

About the Actor:

One of Kevin Spacey's two Oscars was for Best Actor in a Leading Role for *American Beauty* (1999).

"Take your time. I expect to be dead in four."

Bruce Willis as John McClane – **Die Hard With a Vengeance (1995)**

Setting:

McClane's response to Insp. Walter Cobb (Larry Bryggman) when told, "We'll be back to pick you up in fifteen minutes." They had just dropped him off in the middle of Harlem wearing nothing but his boxers and a sign that read, "I Hate Niggers."

Movie Trivia:

On the day of the shoot, they decided to use a sign without the offensive language due to the fact that they actually shot in Harlem and didn't want to cause a riot. Willis wore a sign that said "I hate everyone." The offensive language was put in later with CGI, and the directors and producers hope people understand the language was used to show how evil the bad guy was, not to offend anyone.

About the Actor:

Bruce Willis appeared with Kim Basinger in the comedy *Blind Date* (1987).

"Of course I can. You're all show muscle. Hell, a 120-pound woman hauled you in here in handcuffs. Sit down."

Tom Selleck as Jesse Stone – **Stone Cold (2005)**

Setting:

When Stone tells Bo Marino (Shawn Roberts) he's not walking out of his office, Marino says, "You think you can stop me?" This was Stone's reply. Marino was brought in on a controlled substance charge, but Stone knows the seventeen year old is one of the three who raped a high school girl, and Marino has possessions of photos of the crime that Marino says he "found."

Movie Trivia:

While this was the first Jesse Stone movie, *Stone Cold* is the fourth book in Robert B. Parker's Jesse Stone series.

About the Actor:

Tom Selleck was an Executive Producer for *Stone Cold* (2005), and he says he does not just take the title, but does the work.

"Haven't I told you this is illegal and it pisses me off? You're under arrest."

Dolph Lundren as Sgt. Chris Kenner – **Showdown In Little Tokyo (1991)**

Setting:

Kenner swings down into the ring of an illegal fighting operation to address the organizer. When fighters are told to kick Kenner's ass, one of the crowd calls out, "five grand on the new guy," to which Kenner replies, "that's a good bet."

Movie Trivia:

The tag line for *Showdown In Little Tokyo* (1991) is "One's a warrior. One's a wise guy. They're two L.A. cops going after a gang of Japanese drug lords. Feet first."

About the Actor:

Dolph Lundgren's film debut was in the James Bond feature *A View to a Kill* (1985) starring Roger Moore as James Bond.

"I sure ain't gonna show you my dick."

Sam Elliott as Wade Garrett – **Road House (1989)**

Setting:

Garrett's reply to the tallest of Brad Wesley's (Ben Gazzara) goons when he asks, "Do you want to fight, dickless?"

Movie Trivia:

Road House (1989) was filmed in Valencia, California.

About the Actor:

Sam Elliott's film debut was as Card Player #2 in *Butch Cassidy and the Sundance Kid* (1969).

"Well, then, you just fulfilled the first rule of law enforcement. Make sure when your shift is over you go home alive. Here endeth the lesson."

Sean Connery as Jim Malone – **The Untouchables (1987)**

Setting:

During the first meeting between Eliot Ness (Kevin Costner) and Jim Malone, Malone asks Ness if he wants a free lesson in police work when Ness wants to know how Malone knew he had a gun. When Ness tells Malone he had a rough day on the job and was about to go home, Malone provides his lesson.

Movie Trivia:

The Untouchables (1987) was written by David Mamet, who also was the writer, executive producer, and sometimes director of the television series *The Unit* (2006-2009).

About the Actor:

Sean Connery stated in an interview about *The Untouchables* (1987), "The moment I knew that it was written by Mamet, I was more than interested."

"Meat…or potatoes?"

Robert Downey, Jr. as Sherlock Holmes – **Sherlock Holmes (2009)**

Setting:

Faced with fighting the large Dredger (Robert Maillet) and the two smaller arson accomplices, Holmes asks Dr. John Watson (Jude Law) if he wants Dredger (meat) or the other two (potatoes). Watson replies, "My 10 minutes are up." Earlier, when breaking in, Watson decides to assist Holmes and Holmes states, "It does make a considerable difference to me having someone with me on whom I can thoroughly rely." Watson tells him, "Well, you can rely on me for exactly 10 minutes."

Movie Trivia:

Robert Maillet, who played Dredger, accidently knocked out Robert Downey, Jr. while filming a fight scene.

About the Actor:

Robert Downey, Jr. read many Sherlock Holmes stories and watched *The Adventures of Sherlock Homes* (1984) by Granada Television starring Jeremy Brett in order to learn more about the character.

"I got no problem with killing, Boss. Never have."

Kevin Costner as Charley Waite – **Open Range (2003)**

Setting:

Waite's reply to Boss Spearman (Robert Duvall) when Spearman tells him he aims to kill Baxter (Michael Gambon) and those who killed their man Mose (Abraham Benrubi) and shot the boy Button (Diego Luna).

Movie Trivia:

Abraham Benrubi, who plays Mose in *Open Range* (2003), is widely known as Jerry Markovic, the character he played in the hit television series *ER* (140 episodes, 1994-2009).

About the Actor:

Kevin Michael Costner was born on January 18, 1955, in Lynwood, California.

"Better. No one gets killed."

Liam Neeson as Bryan Mills – **Taken (2008, US release 2009)**

Setting:

Reply to Sam's (Leland Orser) statement, "Okay. It'll be perfect, just like old times," after Mills agrees to help with security for a young rock star's concert.

Movie Trivia:

The ex-agency friends of Bryan Mills were played by actors who had previous roles in spy or cop thriller movies or television shows. Jon Gries (Casey) played a major role in *The Pretender* (1996), Leland Orser (Sam) was in both *The Pretender* (1996) and *24* (2001), and David Warshofsky (Bernie) has appeared in minor roles in numerous similar shows.

About the Actor:

Liam Neeson's birth name was William John Neeson.

"When this is over, remind me to rip Jumbo there's tongue out."

Kurt Russell as Gabe Cash – ***Tango & Cash (1989)***

Setting:

During the trial, Cash leans over and talks to Tango (Sylvester Stallone) about the voice expert who is testifying against them. Tango replies, "With a tow truck."

Movie Trivia:

Albert Magnoli was brought in to replace director Andrei Konchalovsky, and then editor Stuart Baird was brought in during post production by the studio to "rescue" the film.

About the Actor:

Kurt Russell played Packy Kerlin in a 1964 episode of the television series *Gunsmoke* (1964).

"It all comes down to fundamentals."

Eric Roberts as Merle "The Butcher" Henche – **The Butcher (2007)**

Setting:

After killing Doyle (Paul Dillon) and blowing apart his club with a .50 caliber machine gun, Henche pulls one of his gold plated .45s and shoots the last of Doyle's men in the back as he tries to run away. This was his statement before leaving.

Movie Trivia:

The Butcher (2009) was filmed in Los Angeles, California, USA.

About the Actor:

Eric Roberts landed his first leading role in a major film with *King of the Gypsies* (1978).

"I'm the best."

Wesley Snipes as John Cutter – **Passenger 57 (1992)**

Setting:

Cutter's reply to flight attendant Marti Slayton (Alex Datcher) when she asks, "Tell me you're good at this" in regards to Cutter dealing with terrorists.

Movie Trivia:

Alex Datcher, who played flight attendant Marti Slayton, appeared in an episode of *Star Trek: The Next Generation* (1993) as Ensign Zandra Taitt.

About the Actor:

Wesley Snipes is seen reading Sun Tzu's *The Art of War* when the flight attendant is counting passengers. Snipes of course is passenger 57. This was years before Snipes starred in *The Art of War* (2000) and then its sequel *The Art of War II: Betrayal* (2008). Snipes did not reprise his role in *The Art of War III: Retribution* (2009), it starred Anthony 'Treach' Criss.

"Never take your eyes off your opponent."

Bruce Lee as Lee – **Enter the Dragon (1973)**

Setting:

Lee's final lesson to Lahn/Lao (Wei Tung) during their short time near the beginning of the film. When Lahn bows, Lee slaps him in the head and tells him to never take his eyes off his opponent, even when he bows.

Movie Trivia:

Enter the Dragon (1973) was written by Michael Allin, who is also credited as a writer for the movie *Night Train* (2010) starring Sigourney Weaver.

About the Actor:

Brue Lee revised the script for *Enter the Dragon* (1973), including having written and directed the film's opening fight sequence with Samo Hung at the Shaolin Monastery.

"Soylent Green is people! We've got to stop 'em, somehow."

Charlton Heston as Thorn – **Soylent Green (1973)**

Setting:

After Police Detective Thorn fights and shoots his way out of the Soylent Green factory, these final words of the movie disclose his gruesome discovery.

Movie Trivia:

Soylent Green (1973) was Edward G. Robinson's final film. He died of cancer twelve days after shooting his final scene, his death scene, in *Soylent Green* (1973).

About the Actor:

Charlton Heston wrote about Robinson's final scene in his autobiography, *In the Arena*, "It is a very good scene; Eddie is marvelous. As fine an actor as he was, he could hardly have been less, playing that. I was very good too, unconsciously picking up the truth he was exporting. I've never heard of an actor playing a death scene in terms of his own true and imminent death. It was an awesome experience."

"A man needs his exercise."

Patrick Swayze as Nomad – **Steel Dawn (1987)**

Setting:

Nomad's reply to his old teacher, Cord (John Fujioka), when they meet and Cord says, "You've been roaming the wastelands. Brawling with half-men no doubt."

Movie Trivia:

John Fujioka, who played Cord the Peacemaker, appeared in two episodes of *Walker, Texas Ranger* (1993-2001) as Master Rin.

About the Actor:

Patrick Swayze's New York City dance training included the Harkness Ballet School and Joffrey Ballet School.

"I said, put the bunny back in the box."

Nicolas Cage as Cameron Poe – **Con Air (1997)**

Setting:

Convict William 'Billy Bedlam' Bedford (Nick Chinlund) finds Poe's personal items in a box in the cargo area of the plane. Poe tells him the above. He doesn't put the stuffed animal away as Poe directed and the two fight. Poe kills Bedford, and then says to himself, "Why couldn't you put the bunny back in the box?"

Movie Trivia:

Con Air (1997) was the first feature film for Director Simon West. Before this movie, he directed TV commercials.

About the Actor:

Nicholas Kim Coppola was born on January 7, 1964, in Long Beach, California.

"Ain't no room for Peter Pan on this hunt."

Tom Berenger as Thomas Beckett — ***Sniper (1993)***

Setting:

Said to Richard Miller (Billy Zane) right after tossing his "Gucciflage" out the train window as the two travel to their drop point.

Movie Trivia:

Sniper (1993) was written by Michael Frost Beckner and Crash Leyland.

About the Actor:

Tom Berenger's height is listed as 5'11" (1.80m).

"You tell your asshole boss that nobody, nobody threatens me."

Steven Seagal as Lt. Jack Cole – **The Glimmer Man (1996)**

Setting:

Donald Cunningham (John M. Jackson), who heads Frank Deverell's (Bob Gunton) security, comes to the police station to get Cole to testify inaccurately about Deverell's son Johnny (Johnny Strong). This was Cole's reply. After Cunningham says he understands, Cole tells him, "Now get your ugly white ass outta here. And don't come back."

Movie Trivia:

John M. Jackson, who played bad guy Donald Cunningham, also faced Chuck Norris as a bad guy in an episode of *Walker, Texas Ranger* (1998).

About the Actor:

Steven Seagal was recognized by Tibetan Lama Penor Rinpoche as a reincarnated Tulku.

"It'll get worse before it gets better."

Patrick Swayze as Dalton – **Road House (1989)**

Setting:

Dalton's reply to Tilghman (Kevin Tighe) after Dalton's first night working the Double Deuce and firing the bartender, Pat McGurn (John Doe), and Tilghman states, "Well, it was a good night. Nobody died."

Movie Trivia:

David Lee Henry and Hilary Henkin were nominated for a 1990 Razzie Award for Worst Screenplay for *Road House* (1989).

About the Actor:

Two of Patrick Swayze's earlier jobs were working at a Hallmark card store and as a lifeguard at a men's health club.

"Son of a bitch must pay."

Kurt Russell as Jack Burton – ***Big Trouble in Little China (1986)***

Setting:

Said after the guys who snatched Miao Yin (Suzee Pai) try to run him and Wang Chi (Dennis Dun) over in the airport parking garage.

Movie Trivia:

Suzee Pai, who played Miao Yin, had an uncredited part in *First Blood* (1982) with Sylvester Stallone, and debuted as Siakwan in *Sharky's Machine* (1981) with Burt Reynolds.

About the Actor:

Kurt Russell's father, Bing Russell, was a character actor who appeared in many television shows and movies throughout the years.

"Okay, what you know about me could fit in the crack of my ass. I'd just as soon keep it that way."

Steve Austin as John Brickner – **Damage (2009)**

Setting:

Brickner's reply to Reno Paulsaint (Walton Goggins) as Reno tries to convince him to fight for money and says, "Look, I know you're on parole. It can't be easy. Being an ex-con."

Movie Trivia:

Walton Goggins, who plays Reno Paulsaint, appeared as Detective Shane Vendrell in 89 episodes of *The Shield* (2002 – 2008).

About the Actor:

Steve Austin's biological father James Anderson divorced his mother before he had a chance to know him. Austin considers Ken Williams his father, a man he loves and respects.

"I live my life a quarter mile at a time. Nothing else matters. Not the mortgage, not the store, not my team and all their bullshit. For those ten seconds or less, I'm free."

Vin Diesel as Dominic Toretto – **The Fast and the Furious (2001)**

Setting:

Toretto talks with Brian O'Conner (Paul Walker) after showing him his 1970 Dodge Charger. This quote is repeated after the credits when you see Toretto driving in Baja, Mexico.

Movie Trivia:

Toretto's 1970 Dodge Charger is the same body style, but a year newer than the famous 1969 Dodge Charger "General Lee" of *The Dukes of Hazzard* television show.

About the Actor:

Vin Diesel's birth name was Mark Sinclair Vincent.

"Doc, I'll get all the sleep I need when I'm dead."

Sam Elliott as Wade Garrett – **Road House (1989)**

Setting:

Garrett's reply to Doc Elizabeth Clay (Kelly Lynch) when she tells them she is going to get some sleep, and asks, "Aren't you guys tired?"

Movie Trivia:

Blind musician Cody was played by real life blind musician Jeff Healey, who passed away in 2008. The Jeff Healy Band performs numerous songs in the movie and on the soundtrack.

About the Actor:

Sam Elliott's listed height is 6'2" (1.88m).

"Just that fax ma'am. Just the fax."

Bruce Willis as Lt. John McClane – **Die Hard 2 Die Harder (1990)**

Setting:

After she assists McClane with a fax, the attendant tells him, "Say, I close in about an hour. Maybe we can go get a drink?" He holds up his finger and shows her his wedding band and makes the spoof on the famous *Dragnet* line.

Movie Trivia:

While "Just the facts, ma'am" has come to be known as *Dragnet's* catch phrase, it was never actually uttered by Joe Friday (Jack Webb).

About the Actor:

Bruce Willis, along with fellow actors Tom Selleck, Arnold Schwarzenegger, and John Milius, is one of the few outspoken conservatives in Hollywood. Dennis Hopper was also in that group.

"Pride's a weakness."

Mel Gibson as Benjamin Martin – ***The Patriot (2000)***

Setting:

After reading the journals of Gen. Lord Charles Cornwallis (Tom Wilkinson), Martin discusses strategy with his men in the swamp. Martin acknowledges Cornwallis is a genius when it comes to war, but that he also knows it. Maybe pride is his weakness.

Movie Trivia:

The Patriot (2000) was written by Robert Rodat. Rodat also wrote *Saving Private Ryan* (1998).

About the Actor:

Mel Gibson was awarded the AO (Officer of the Order of Australia), Australia's highest honor, in 1997.

"My name's Briar Gates. I want the man who killed my brother. Let's put our thinking caps on boys, I don't have all night."

Liam Neeson as Briar Gates – **Next of Kin (1989)**

Setting:

Briar Gates confronts Joey Rosselina (Adam Baldwin) and others with a shotgun while looking for his brother's killer. After shooting up the place, he asks, "How's the memory doing now, boys?" When Joey tells him he just made the worst mistake of his life, he replies, "No sir, I think you did." His parting words, "Fair warning boys, when I find out who killed my brother, working around here is just gonna be no fun at all."

Movie Trivia:

Next of Kin (1989) was directed by John Irvin, who also directed *Raw Deal* (1986) with Arnold Schwarzenegger, among many other films.

About the Actor:

Next of Kin (1989) is one of a number of movies where Liam Neeson's character has died. His character's dying words to brother Truman, played by Patrick Swayze, "Should've waited for you. We coulda wupped them together."

"You pull on me, either of you, I'll kill you both."

Ed Harris as Virgil Cole – **Appaloosa (2008)**

Setting:

Cole and Hitch (Viggo Mortensen) confront Randall Bragg's (Jeremy Irons) men in the saloon just after they are appointed the law in Appaloosa. The men don't believe him, and one draws, so Cole does what he says he would. When the shocked town leaders come in and see the bodies, Cole says, "I warned them."

Movie Trivia:

Appaloosa (2008) was written by Robert Knott and Ed Harris, who had a hand in just about everything with this film. The screenplay was based on Robert B. Parker's novel.

About the Actor:

Ed Harris directed and was also listed as one of the producers of *Appaloosa* (2008).

"You want to talk to God? Let's go see Him together. I've got nothing better to do."

Harrison Ford as Indiana Jones – **Raiders of the Lost Ark (1981)**

Setting:

Indy confronts Belloq (Paul Freeman) in a tavern at Belloq's request while Indy is drinking because he believes Marion was in the truck that blew up. The conversation started with Indy saying, "I ought to kill you right now." It ended with a bunch of kids coming in and stopping Indy from drawing his gun after the quote above.

Movie Trivia:

Paul Freeman, who played Belloq, has a long string of television roles including Dr. Charles Corday, Dr. Elizabeth Corday's (Alex Kingston) father, in three episodes of the popular television series *ER* (1994 – 2009).

About the Actor:

Harrison Ford received a star on Hollywood Walk of Fame in 2003.

"I guess I'm not trained for this."

Steven Seagal as Casey Ryback – **Under Siege 2: Dark Territory (1995)**

Setting:

Ryback meets his niece, Sarah Ryback (Katherine Heigl), at the train station to go with her to California by train after her parents have been killed in a plane crash. He has not seen her in many years, and he brought her a teddy bear, something she has outgrown. This quote sets up a later quote when terrorists take over the train, something Ryback is trained for.

Movie Trivia:

Katherine Heigl, who played Seagal's niece Sarah, is more widely known for her roll as Alison Scott in the comedy *Knocked Up* (2007) with Seth Rogen.

About the Actor:

Steven Seagal was also credited as a producer of *Under Siege 2: Dark Territory* (1995).

"You going to do something or just stand there and bleed?"

Kurt Russell as Wyatt Earp – **Tombstone (1993)**

Setting:

After telling the faro dealer at the Oriental Saloon, Johnny Tyler (Billy Bob Thornton), "No need to go heeled to get the bulge on a devil like you." Tyler asks, "Is that a fact?" Earp replies, "That's a fact." Tyler stands and says, "Well, I'm real scared." Earp says, "You're damn right you're scared. I can see that in your eyes. Go ahead. Go ahead, skin it. Skin that smoke wagon and see what happens." Earp then slaps him around before escorting him out of the saloon and taking over the faro table.

Movie Trivia:

In 1993, Billy Bob Thornton appeared in *Living and Working in Space: The Countdown Has Begun* (1993), *Trouble Bound* (1993), *Grey Knight* (1993), *Indecent Proposal* (1993), *Bound by Honor* (1993), and *Tombstone* (1993).

About the Actor:

Kurt Russell was born on March 17, 1951.

"You know all those goddamn security scenarios we ran? Well, I'm stuck in the middle of one we didn't think of."

Samuel L. Jackson as Neville Flynn – ***Snakes on a Plane (2006)***

Setting:

FBI Agent Flynn reports to Agent Harris (Bobby Cannavale), by phone, that Eddie Kim (Byron Lawson) managed to fill the plane with poisonous snakes.

Movie Trivia:

When air steward Ken (Bruce James) throws a snake into the microwave, he pushes the preset button labeled "snakes" to fry it.

About the Actor:

Samuel L. Jackson graduated from Morehouse College in Atlanta, GA, in 1972.

"They say if you must resort to violence, then you've already lost. What do you think Jeff?"

Sean Connery as Capt. John Connor – **Rising Sun (1993)**

Setting:

After Capt. Connor puts Jeff's (James Oliver Bullock) fellow bodyguard Perry (Tony Ganios) to the ground with a single strike to the throat, he turns to Jeff and poses the above question. Jeff's reply, "I think I'll go get Mr. Sakamura."

Movie Trivia:

Eddie Sakamura's red car is a Vector W8, an American-made supercar manufactured by Vector Aeromotive and produced from 1989 to 1993.

About the Actor:

No Road Back (1957) was Sean Connery's first major movie role. Connery played Spike, a gang member, in his brief supporting role in the otherwise forgettable crime drama.

"All right, which one of you is the ugliest most inbred country son-of-a-bitch out here?"

Tommy Lee Jones as Chief Deputy Marshal Samuel Gerard – ***U.S. Marshals (1998)***

Setting:

Gerard is picking a local to guide his boat as they hit the swamps to track Mark J. Sheridan (Wesley Snipes). He asks this when everyone raised their hand to his first question, "Which one of you knows the most about this terrain?"

Movie Trivia:

It's reported that Wesley Snipes disliked shooting scenes where he is in water (of which there are two) because he doesn't swim.

About the Actor:

Tommy Lee Jones was nominated for Best Actor in a Supporting Role for *JFK* (1991). Jack Palance won that year for *City Slickers* (1991).

"Ah, you know, nothing I'm not used to. But it's amazing what you can get used to, huh?"

Patrick Swayze as Dalton – **Road House (1989)**

Setting:

Dalton's reply to Garrett (Sam Elliott) when he asks over the phone, "You having trouble?' Then Garrett replies, "Yeah, tell me about it. This place has a sign hanging over the urinal that says, 'Don't eat the big white mint.'"

Movie Trivia:

In one scene, Dalton is reading *Legends of the Fall* by Jim Harrison.

About the Actor:

Growing up, Patrick Swayze, like his father, went by the name "Buddy." When his father was around he went by the name "Little Buddy."

"How could I forget about you? You're the only person I know."

Matt Damon as Jason Bourne – **The Bourne Identity (2002)**

Setting:

After Marie (Franka Potente) gives Bourne a ride, he says she can come up to his apartment and wait, and she tells him, "No, with you, you would probably just forget about me if I stayed here." This is his reply.

Movie Trivia:

The screenplay for *The Bourne Identity* (2002) was written by Tony Gilroy and William Blake Herron based on the novel by Robert Ludlum.

About the Actor:

Matthew Paige Damon was born on October 8, 1970.

"Why don't you button up your britches and go home."

Gregory Peck as Jimmy Ringo – **The Gunfighter (1950)**

Setting:

Said to Eddie (Richard Jaeckel) in the opening bar scene as Eddie tries to show how tough he is by calling Jimmy Ringo out. Ringo tries to avoid the fight by saying, "Now listen pardner, I come in here minding my own business, now how about letting me go out the same way." Eddie presses it and draws on Ringo. It was the last thing Eddie ever did.

Movie Trivia:

Richard Jaeckel, who played Eddie, was diagnosed with cancer in 1996, the same time his wife had Alzheimer's. The Jaeckels had lost their Brentwood, CA, home and were over $1 million in debt. After his family was unsuccessful at getting him into the Motion Picture and Television Hospital in Woodland Hills, CA, Peck lobbied for his "admittance" and he was placed in the facility. He stayed in the hospital until he died in June, 1997.

About the Actor:

Eldred Gregory Peck was born on April 5, 1916, in La Jolla, California. He died on June 12, 2003.

"I'm too old for this shit."

Danny Glover as Sergeant Roger Murtaugh – **Lethal Weapon (1987)**

Setting:

Murtaugh notices his soon-to-be-partner outside his office, and not knowing Riggs (Mel Gibson) is a fellow cop, reacts to Riggs having a gun, ending up on the floor looking up at his new partner. The is the first of several times Murtaugh says this line.

Movie Trivia:

Screen writer Shane Black was 22 years old when he sold the screenplay for *Lethal Weapon* (1987).

About the Actor:

Danny Glover was actually 40 years old when *Lethal Weapon* (1987) was filmed, though his character, Sergeant Roger Murtaugh celebrated his 50th birthday at the beginning of the film.

"And you, music lover, you're next."

Val Kilmer as Doc Holliday – **Tombstone (1993)**

Setting:

As Wyatt Earp (Kurt Russell) holds a gun to Ike Clanton's (Stephen Lang) head and tells the crowd to leave, Holliday comes out of the saloon and points his gun at Billy Clanton (Thomas Haden Church), who is thinking of rushing Earp, and says the above. Holliday and Billy Clanton had previously had an exchange in the saloon over the piece Holliday was playing on the piano. Clanton tells Holliday, "You're so drunk you can't hit nothing. In fact, you're probably seeing double." Holliday pulls out another gun and replies, "I have two guns, one for each of you."

Movie Trivia:

The nocturne played by Doc Holliday is Chopin's Nocturne in E minor, Op. 72, No. 1.

About the Actor:

Val Kilmer's height is listed as 6' (1.83 m).

"Alright Bernard, which is it gonna be, drive your car into the lake, or get a dislocated elbow?"

Tom Laughlin as Billy Jack – **Billy Jack (1971)**

Setting:

When Billy finds Bernard (David Roya) in his car with the girl he just forced by knife to remove her top, he tells him, "Okay Bernard, get out of the car and let's teach you a lesson that your daddy should have taught you a long time ago." However, Jean (Delores Taylor) has a different idea, so Billy gives Bernard a choice between Jean's way or his way to learn the lesson.

Movie Trivia:

In an interview, Tom Laughlin gives credit to his son, Frank, for the line, "drive your car into the lake or get a dislocated elbow."

About the Actor:

Tom Laughlin is the author *of 9 Indispensable Ingredients to Writing a Hit*, also released as *Tom Laughlin's 9 Secrets to Writing a Hit*. The book is advertised for anyone wanting to write a movie, TV show, play, or novel.

"Not quite yet. We haven't heard from your friend here."

Alan Ladd as Shane – **Shane (1953)**

Setting:

Shane's reply to Ryker (Emile Meyer) when he says, "All right. So we all turn in our sixguns to the bartender. And we'll all start hoeing spuds, is that it?" Shane motions to gunfighter Jack Wilson (Jack Palance) sitting alone at a table in the bar.

Movie Trivia:

Director and Producer, George Stevens, was nominated for two 1954 Oscars for Best Director and Best Picture. These were two of 6 nominations, with the only win going for the 1954 Oscar for Best Cinematography, Color, to Loyal Griggs.

About the Actor:

Alan Ladd has a star on the Hollywood Walk of Fame at 1601 Vine Street.

"Of course I'm afraid. You think I'm reluctant because I'm happy?"

Robert De Niro as Sam – ***Ronin (1998)***

Setting:

After evaluating the men who possess the case they are going to steal, Sam says they need more men to do the job. Deirdre (Natascha McElhone) replies, "There's no more help. There's no more men. Are you afraid?" This was Sam's reply.

Movie Trivia:

In an interview, Stunt-Car Coordinator Jean-Claude Lagniez said the Paris Chief of Police said they could do what they wanted, with no restrictions. Lagniez says that was exceptional.

About the Actor:

Robert De Niro married his second wife, Grace Hightower, in 1997. They have one son, Elliot De Niro, born on March 18, 1998.

"I don't think you understand. These boys killed my dog."

Mark Wahlberg as Bob Lee Swagger – **Shooter (2007)**

Setting:

After Swagger shoots the three men who are about to help Special Agent Nick Memphis (Michael Pena) kill himself with a suicide harness, Memphis tries to convince Swagger to turn himself in so things can be worked out. This is Swagger explaining his reasoning.

Movie Trivia:

Michael Pena, who played Nick Memphis, also appeared as Detective Armando Renta in the television series *The Shield* (2005).

About the Actor:

Mark Wahlberg's older brother Donnie Wahlberg was a member of the popular 1980s group New Kids on the Block. Mark was also an original member, but backed out early on.

"Well, enjoy it. Because once it starts, it's gonna be messy like nothing you ever seen."

Kevin Costner as Charley Waite – **Open Range (2003)**

Setting:

Waite's reply to Boss Spearman (Robert Duvall) after Spearman comments that it's a pretty day for making things right; just before the final gunfight against Denton Baxter (Michael Gambon) and his men.

Movie Trivia:

The tag line for *Open Range* (2003) is "No place to run. No reason to hide."

About the Actor:

Kevin Costner is a member of the Delta Chi Fraternity.

"Hooray for the sounds of fuckin' silence."

Nicolas Cage as Cameron Poe – **Con Air (1997)**

Setting:

Poe runs into a group of drug dealers with their jet while looking for insulin and syringes for his friend O'Dell (Mykelti Williamson). He tells the criminal holding the gun if he fires, 20 pissed off prisoners will hear it. The guy puts a silencer on his weapon, prompting this quote.

Movie Trivia:

Con Air (1997) was written by Scott Rosenberg, who also wrote the screenplay for *Gone in Sixty Seconds* (2000) also starring Nicolas Cage.

About the Actor:

Nicolas Cage's father, August Coppola, was a brother of director Francis Ford Coppola.

"Yeah. I heard that too."

Bruce Willis as Lt. John McClane – **Die Hard 2 Die Harder (1990)**

Setting:

McClane's reply when he is reunited with his wife, Holly (Bonnie Bedelia), and she says, "They told me there were terrorists at the airport."

Movie Trivia:

Bonnie Bedelia plays Holly McClane in the first two *Die Hard* movies, but is absent from volumes 3 and 4 of the series.

About the Actor:

Bruce Willis took a 3 percent stake in struggling French drinks company Belvedere in exchange for endorsing its flagship vodka brand Sobieski.

"Never ain't here yet."

Ed Harris as Virgil Cole – **Appaloosa (2008)**

Setting:

Cole's reply to Randall Bragg (Jeremy Irons) after Ring Shelton (Lance Henriksen) and Mackie Shelton (Adam Nelson) use Allison French (Renee Zellweger) to get Cole to release Bragg from the train they were transporting him on. Bragg told Cole, "I told you you'd never hang me, Cole."

Movie Trivia:

It's reported that Diane Lane was originally cast as Allison French. She left the project during pre-production. Renee Zellweger did a fine job in the role.

About the Actor:

Ed Harris is listed as 5' 9" (1.75 m) tall.

"I may not live long Eddie, but I'm living longer than you."

Eric Roberts as Merle "The Butcher" Henche – **The Butcher (2007)**

Setting:

Eddie Hellstrom (Jerry Trimble, Jr.) sends Henche to the Spearmint Rhino to collect money. While there, Henche exits the restroom and runs into Eddie who is holding a gun and wearing a mask. He and three others are robbing the place. Eddie tells Henche, "Good idea to rob the place. Too bad you get shot in the process." When Eddie looks away, Henche pulls his revolver and shoots Eddie between the eyes and says the above.

Movie Trivia:

Jerry Trimble, who played Eddie, appeared as Knox Thug in *Charlie's Angels* (2000).

About the Actor:

Eric Roberts starred with Mickey Rourke in *The Pope of Greenwich Village* (1984).

Alain Burrese

"Not even God knows what you're doing!"

Samuel L. Jackson as Zeus Carver – **Die Hard With a Vengeance (1995)**

Setting:

Carver's reply when he and McClane (Bruce Willis) are arguing in the cab regarding the best route to take and McClane says, "Would you stop that goddamn yelling. I know what I'm doing."

Movie Trivia:

Samuel L. Jackson and Bruce Willis worked together a year before this film when they both appeared in *Pulp Fiction* (1994).

About the Actor:

Samuel L. Jackson worked as a camera stand-in for Bill Cosby during the filming of *The Cosby Show* (1984).

"Outside."

Bruce Lee as Lee – **Enter the Dragon (1973)**

Setting:

While Lee is practicing in his room, Oharra (Bob Wall) opens the door and tells him, "You must attend the morning ritual in uniform." This was Lee's one word response, commanding Oharra to leave his room, made more impressive as he holds his leg up in the side kick position during the exchange.

Movie Trivia:

In 2004, *Enter the Dragon* (1973) was deemed "Culturally Significant" and selected for preservation in the National Film Registry.

About the Actor:

Bruce Lee played Kato in 26 episodes of *The Green Hornet* (1966-1967) and 3 episodes of *Batman* (1966-1967).

"Lucky for me, this place is soundproof. That way nobody gets to hear me beating the truth out of you."

Kurt Russell as Gabe Cash – ***Tango & Cash (1989)***

Setting:

Cash confronts Skinner (Michael Jeter), the person who doctored the tape to set him and Tango (Sylvester Stallone) up, after escaping from prison.

Movie Trivia:

Billy Blanks, of Tae-Bo fame as well as other movies, has an uncredited role as a prison thug.

About the Actor:

Kurt Russell is the ex-brother-in-law of Larry J. Franco, who was a co-producer of *Tango & Cash* (1989).

"Wrong choice."

Dwayne "The Rock" Johnson as Beck – ***The Rundown (2003)***

Setting:

In the nightclub, Beck gives Knappmiller (Stephen Bishop) two choices, "Option 'A' you give me the ring. Option 'B' I make you give me the ring." He chooses 'B' and Beck says the above and starts cleaning house.

Movie Trivia:

Dwayne "The Rock" Johnson uses his signature wrestling move the Rock Bottom on one of the thugs in the nightclub fight.

About the Actor:

Dwayne Johnson's cousin, Tanoai Reed, was his stunt double for *The Rundown* (2003). He won a Taurus Award for Best Overall Stunt by a Stunt Man at the World Stunt Awards for the scene when two stunt men are thrown from a jeep as it falls off the side of a cliff.

"Excuse me. I'm collecting for the local blood bank, anyone care to make a donation? (I left my wallet in my locker – football player) Well, I wasn't talking about money."

Treat Williams as Karl Thomasson – **The Substitute 3: Winner Takes All (1999)**

Setting:

Thomasson interrupts three football players who are harassing Prof. Nicole Stewart (Rebecca Staab) in a pizza restaurant. He then proceeds to help them with their blood donations by kicking butt all over the place.

Movie Trivia:

The Substitute 3: Winner Takes All (1999) was directed by Robert Radler, who also directed *Best of the Best* (1989) and *Best of the Best 2* (1993).

About the Actor:

Treat Williams cinematic breakthrough was as George Berger in the movie version of the popular musical *Hair* (1979).

"Don't try this at home, boys and girls."

Mel Gibson as Sergeant Martin Riggs – **Lethal Weapon 2 (1989)**

Setting:

Riggs dislocates his shoulder in order to get out of a straitjacket to win a bet with fellow police officers. When asked why he does such things to himself by the department psychiatrist, Dr. Stephanie Woods (Mary Ellen Trainor), he replies, "Well, who else could I do it to, I mean none of them will let me. And besides, I need the money."

Movie Trivia:

This scene is the first time we see Riggs dislocate his shoulder, something he does later in this movie, and something that happens in the next two movies as well.

About the Actor:

Mel Gibson married Robyn Moore in 1980, and the two filed for divorce in 2009.

"It ain't about trust, it's about survival."

Steven Seagal as Shane Daniels – **A Dangerous Man (2009)**

Setting:

After Sergey (Jesse Hutch) drops Daniels and Tia (Marlaina Mah) off at a motel, Daniels walks to a different one saying, "If they catch that kid, we're fucked. From him they'll roll back to that other motel. You understand?" She replies, "You don't trust anyone, do you?" This was his answer.

Movie Trivia:

Jesse Hutch, who plays Sergey, has a long list of television credits, including: *Dark Angel* (2001), *American Dreams* (2002 – 2004), Smallville (2002 – 2005), *About a Girl* (2007 – 2008), and *Kyle XY* (2009).

About the Actor:

While working with Sean Connery for the movie *Never Say Never Again* (1983), it is reported that Steven Seagal broke Connery's wrist.

"And then some."

Bruce Willis as Joe Hallenbeck – **The Last Boy Scout (1991)**

Setting:

Hallenbeck's reply to the pimp looking thug in the alley who calls him a bastard as he's dying. The thug was going to shoot Hallenbeck, but Hallenbeck tells some fat jokes and then slices the thug's neck with a bottle when he's laughing.

Movie Trivia:

Hallenbeck also says this line when he kicks Jimmy Dix (Damon Wayans) out of his house for using drugs.

About the Actor:

In the late 1980s, Bruce Willis recorded an album of pop-blues titled *The Return of Bruno*, which author Alain Burrese still owns on cassette which he purchased when it first came out.

"Yes, I do."

Tommy Lee Jones as Chief Deputy Marshal Samuel Gerard – **U.S. Marshals (1998)**

Setting:

As Gerard gets into an elevator after telling Deputy Marshal Cosmo Renfro (Joe Pantoliano) he's going after Mark J. Sheridan (Wesley Snipes) alone, Cosmo says, "The Great Sam Gerard." Gerard replies, "Yes, I am." Then Cosmo says, "And you always have to win." This was his reply.

Movie Trivia:

The marshals' offices were the exact same building and floor used in *The Fugitive* (1993). They were shot on the 20th floor of 444 North Michigan Ave. in Chicago.

About the Actor:

Tommy Lee Jones received a B.A. in English Literature and graduated cum laude from Harvard University in 1969.

"Their idea of combat is tearing up the countryside with heavy artillery and millions of rounds. We'll wait days for one shot, one kill."

Tom Berenger as Thomas Beckett – **Sniper (1993)**

Setting:

Upon meeting Richard Miller (Billy Zane), Becket explains the differences between regular soldiers and snipers, who he calls, "an outcast profession."

Movie Trivia:

Sniper (1993) was directed by Luis Llosa, who also directed *The Specialist* (1994) starring Sylvester Stallone.

About the Actor:

Tom Berenger's birth name was Thomas Michael Moore.

"The ones who go looking for trouble are not much of a problem to someone who's ready for them. I suspect it's always been that way."

Patrick Swayze as Dalton – **Road House (1989)**

Setting:

In the café, Dalton explains to Elizabeth Clay (Kelly Lynch) why he's always been better and hasn't been put down as she asks him questions. When she says somebody has to do it, he replies, "Somebody's got to pay somebody to do it."

Movie Trivia:

In the same year, Kelly Lynch appeared in *Road House* (1989), *Warm Summer Rain* (1989), *Drugstore Cowboy* (1989), and *The Edge* (1989) (TV).

About the Actor:

In *The Time of My Life*, Patrick Swayze says his father taught him to fight, but also told him, "If I ever see you start a fight, I'll kick your ass. And if I ever see you not *finish* a fight, I'll kick your ass."

"You slow down, dickhead. I'm the one who's dying."

Kurt Russell as Snake Plissken – ***Escape From L.A. (1996)***

Setting:

As Snake Plissken speeds toward L.A. in the speed submarine, Cmdr. Mallow (Stacy Keach) tells Snake over the radio, "Hey, watch your speed, hot shot. There's lots of obstructions down there…Slow it down, Plissken. You're overloading the power plant." This is Plissken's reply.

Movie Trivia:

In the first movie, everyone thought Plissken was dead. In this one, the repeating joke is people thinking he'd be taller.

About the Actor:

Kurt Russell's persistence helped get *Escape From L.A.* (1996) made. He wanted to play the character Snake Plissken again.

"You want Capone? Here's how you get him: He pulls a knife, you pull a gun. He sends one of yours to the hospital, you send one of his to the morgue. That's the Chicago way! And that's how you get Capone."

Sean Connery as Jim Malone – ***The Untouchables (1987)***

Setting:

Malone asks Ness (Kevin Costner) if he is ready to do anything to get Capone while talking privately in a church. Malone offers to help Ness and tells him the above and that he just took a blood oath when Ness agrees. Later, when one of the Canadian Mounties says he does not approve of his methods, Ness replies, "Yeah? Well, you're not from Chicago."

Movie Trivia:

The Untouchables (1987) was directed by Brian De Palma, who also directed *Carrie* (1976) and *Scarface* (1983), among other hits.

About the Actor:

Sean Connery spent time as a coffin polisher in Edinburgh.

"I have come here to chew bubblegum and kick ass … and I'm all out of bubblegum."

"Rowdy" Roddy Piper as Nada – ***They Live (1988)***

Setting:

Nada enters a bank shortly after discovering the sunglasses that reveal the aliens and acquiring weapons from the alien police officers that tried to take him in. He lets loose on the aliens in the bank.

Movie Trivia:

According to Director John Carpenter, Piper ad-libbed the line "I have come here to chew bubblegum and kick ass, and I'm all out of bubblegum." It came from a list of ideas from his professional wrestling interviews.

About the Actor:

Roderick George Toombs, aka Roddy Piper, was born April 17, 1954, in Saskatoon, Saskatchewan, Canada.

"Yeah, well … I also cook."

Steven Seagal as Casey Ryback – **Under Siege (1992)**

Setting:

Ryback's reply to Jordan Tate (Erika Eleniak) when she states, "You're not a cook." Earlier, former SEAL Ryback told Tate he was just a cook when she asked if he was a special forces guy or something.

Movie Trivia:

Erika Eleniak's character, Jordan Tate, is the July 1989 Playmate who was hired to jump out of a cake. In reality, Erika Eleniak actually was the July 1989 Playmate.

About the Actor:

Steven Seagal's height is reported to be 6'4" (1.93 m).

"Because your idea of cooperation is me in a cell, and I don't particularly like that."

Wesley Snipes as Neil Shaw – ***The Art of War (2000)***

Setting:

As the police raid the gentleman's club, Shaw confronts FBI Agent Frank Capella (Maury Chaykin) outside near the car with Julia Fang (Marie Matiko). Capella says, "We're both after the same thing. Why can't we work together on this?" This is Shaw's reason.

Movie Trivia:

The Art of War (2000) was directed by Christian Duguay.

About the Actor:

Wesley Snipes' first wife was April Dubois. They were married from 1985 to 1990 and had one child, Jelani Asar Snipes (born 1988).

"Get off my plane."

Harrison Ford as President James Marshall – **Air Force One (1997)**

Setting:

President Marshall's final words to terrorist Ivan Korshunov (Gary Oldman) before Korshunov's neck is broken and he is sucked out of the back of Air Force One, the President's plane, when Marshall opens Korshunov's parachute after wrapping a strap around his neck.

Movie Trivia:

Air Force One (1997) was nominated for two Oscars, Best Film Editing (Richard Francis-Bruce) and Best Sound (Paul Massey, Rick Kline, Doug Hemphill, and Keith A. Wester).

About the Actor:

Harrison Ford told Gary Oldman to actually hit him during the filming of the fight scenes in *Air Force One* (1997).

"Hate is not the answer."

Phillip Rhee as Tommy Lee – **Best of the Best 3: No Turning Back (1995)**

Setting:

After beating Donnie Hansen (Mark Rolston) in the final fight, Hansen tells Tommy Lee to kill him and that he hates the world. This is Tommy Lee's reply as he drives his knife into the ground next to Hansen's head.

Movie Trivia:

The screenplay for *Best of the Best 3: No Turning Back* (1995) was written by Barry Gray and Deborah Scott.

About the Actor:

Phillip Rhee directed *Best of the Best 3: No Turning Back* (1995).

"Very good, but brick not hit back."

Bolo Yeung as Chong Li – **Bloodsport (1988)**

Setting:

Chong Li Comments after seeing Frank Dux (Jean-Claude Van Damme) demonstrate *dim mak* (death touch) by shattering the bottom brick of a stack of bricks he strikes in order to prove his instructor was Tanaka (Roy Chiao), and gain entry into the *Kumite*.

Movie Trivia:

Bolo Yeung delivers a line similar to the line Bruce Lee stated when Bob Wall tried to impress him by breaking boards in *Enter the Dragon* (1973). Lee's line was "Boards don't hit back." Bolo Yeung had a memorable role in *Enter the Dragon* (1973), even though he had no spoken lines.

About the Actor:

Bolo Yeung was born on July 3, 1946, in Canton, China, which made him 42 years old the year *Bloodsport* (1988) was released.

"You ever thought about being a professional singer? Don't."

Patrick Swayze as Jack Crews – ***Black Dog (1998)***

Setting:

Crews kicking Earl (Randy Travis) out of the cab to ride in the follow car, while Sonny (Gabriel Casseus) rides in the truck with him. Earlier, Earl had been singing a song he was working on while riding with Crews.

Movie Trivia:

Randy Travis, who plays Earl, is actually a country music superstar turned part-time actor. His song, "My Greatest Fear" is featured on the *Black Dog* (1998) soundtrack. Also on the soundtrack is "On Down the Line" by Patty Loveless. Author Alain Burrese saw Randy Travis and Patty Loveless together at Camp Red Cloud, near Uijongbu, South Korea, during their 1988 USO tour.

About the Actor:

Patrick Swayze had a classic moment on *Saturday Night Live* (1990) when he lost a Chippendales dance off to Chris Farley.

"You found me in quite an unpleasant mood this morning, mate. Now, I'm gonna ask you this question one time. Who's gots my fucking strawberry tart?"

Jason Statham as Chev Chelios – **Crank 2: High Voltage (2009)**

Setting:

With his shotgun shoved up a very uncomfortable place, Chelios asks a thug (Setu Taase) who has his heart (strawberry tart), shortly after it had been replaced with an artificial temporary one. After he learns Johnny Vang (Art Hsu) has his heart and where Vang is, he tells the guy, regarding the shotgun still stuck in a certain orifice, "Now, you can keep that."

Movie Trivia:

Crank 2: High Voltage (2009) was written and directed by the team of Mark Neveldine and Brian Taylor.

About the Actor:

Jason Statham was an Olympic Diver on the British National Diving Team and finished 12th in the World Championships in 1992.

"You'll kill her. And then I'll kill you. Just like that. I'm ichin' to kill somebody, so it might just as well be you."

Tom Laughlin as Billy Jack – ***Billy Jack (1971)***

Setting:

Billy rides up on horseback with his rifle after Martin escapes from Stuart Posner (Bert Freed) and his men, but is being chased by Bernard Posner (David Roya) who kills him. Deputy Mike (Ken Tobey) pulls his gun and points it at Cindy's (Susan Foster) head. He tells Billy, "Now you drop that gun or I'll shoot her. I'm not gonna ask you again." Billy tells him, "You won't have to." When Mike asks, "What?" Billy replies, "I said shoot her." Mike then says, "You'd kill her just like that, huh?" Billy responded with the above.

Movie Trivia:

Starting in the 1940s, through the 1980s, Bert Freed appeared in numerous movies and television shows, including: *The Untouchables* (1960), *Perry Mason* (1960-1964), *The Munsters* (1965), *Combat* (1965), *Gunsmoke* (1959-1965), *Hogan's Heroes* (1966), *Get Smart* (1966), *Shane* (1966), *The Green Hornet* (1967), *Tarzan* (1967), *Mission Impossible* (1969-1972), *The Partridge Family* (1972), *Knight Rider* (1983), and *The Fall Guy* (1982-1984).

About the Actor:

Tom Laughlin and Delores Taylor have three children: Frank, Teresa, and Christina.

"If I stay drunk, I won't kill anything."

Jean-Claude Van Damme as Eddie Lomax – **Desert Heat (1999)**

Setting:

Lomax's reply to Johnny Six Toes (Danny Trejo) as Johnny nurses Lomax back to health and Lomax picks up a bottle. Johnny says, "See you still like your tequila."

Movie Trivia:

Danny Trejo is not the only familiar face in *Desert Heat* (1999). The movie also features Pat Morita, Silas Weir Mitchell, Jaime Pressley, and Bill Erwin among the cast.

About the Actor:

Jean-Claude Van Damme is also known as "The Muscles from Brussels."

"No Father, I'm praying for Vengeance."

Gary Busey as Buck Matthews – ***Eye of the Tiger (1986)***

Setting:

Matthews replies to Father Healey (Bert Remsen) after he asks, "We are praying for the soul of your wife?"

Movie Trivia:

The name of the movie comes from the theme song "Eye of the Tiger" by Survivor that was made famous as the theme song for Sylvester Stallone's *Rocky III* (1982). It was quite a surprise to hear "Rocky" music in this Gary Busey action movie.

About the Actor:

Gary Busey appeared in an episode of *Kung Fu* with David Carradine in 1973. Busey and Carradine last appeared together in the movie *Blizhniy Boy: The Ultimate fighter* (2007) that also featured Cung Li, Eric Roberts, Bolo Yeung, and Oleg Taktarov.

"I was born ready."

Kurt Russell as Jack Burton – **Big Trouble in Little China (1986)**

Setting:

Burton and Wang Chi (Dennis Dun) are outside in the rain about to go into the Wing Kong Trading Co. to rescue Miao Yin (Suzee Pai). Burton tells Wang Chi, "This is gonna take crackerjack timing, Wang." This is how Jack responds when Chi replies, "Total concentration. You ready Jack?"

Movie Trivia:

Dennis Dun, who played Wang Chi, debuted in *Year of the Dragon* (1985). *Big Trouble in Little China* (1986) was his second movie role.

About the Actor:

Kurt Russell played Elvis Presley and his father, Bing Russell, played Vernon Presley in *Elvis* (1979).

"This ain't no game, Flash. Real Guns. Real bullets. It's dangerous."

Bruce Willis as Joe Hallenbeck – **The Last Boy Scout (1991)**

Setting:

Hallenbeck tells Jimmy Dix (Damon Wayans) that going after more evidence and those that killed Dix's girlfriend, Cory (Halle Berry), isn't a game. Dix replies, "Danger's my middle name." Hallenbeck tells him, "Mine's Cornelius. Tell anybody, I'll kill you."

Movie Trivia:

The Last Boy Scout (1991) was directed by Tony Scott, who also directed *Top Gun* (1986), *Beverly Hills Cop II* (1987), *Days of Thunder* (1990), *Spy Game* (2001), and *Man on Fire* (2004), among others.

About the Actor:

Bruce Willis filled in for an ill David Letterman on his show February 26, 2003, when he was supposed to be a guest.

"This is God's house. Don't make me do this."

Steven Seagal as Lt. Jack Cole – **The Glimmer Man (1996)**

Setting:

Cole confronts Christopher Maynard (Stephen Tobolowsky) in a church. Maynard wants Cole to kill him to put him out of his pain and points his gun at Cole, demanding Cole shoot him, but Cole doesn't want it to end that way. Unfortunately, it does.

Movie Trivia:

The Glimmer Man (1996) was directed by John Gray.

About the Actor:

Steven Seagal's father, Stephen, was a math teacher.

"Feelings get you killed."

Ed Harris as Virgil Cole – **Appaloosa (2008)**

Setting:

Sitting at the campfire, on the trail of the men who have Allison French (Renee Zellweger), Cole tells Everett Hitch (Viggo Mortensen), "The reason you ain't as good as the Sheltons or me ain't got nothing to do with steady or fast or fortuitous. The reason the above-named folks are better than you is because you got feelings." Cole continues with the above quote.

Movie Trivia:

The quote from the movie "Feelings get you killed" is also the film's tagline.

About the Actor:

Edward Allen Harris was born on November 28, 1950, in Tenafly, New Jersey.

"Yeah. I once removed a guy's appendix with a grapefruit spoon."

Robert De Niro as Sam – ***Ronin (1998)***

Setting:

As Sam gets ready to direct the removal of the bullet from his own side, Vincent (Jean Reno) asks, "Are you sure you can do this?" This is Sam's reply.

Movie Trivia:

The tag line for *Ronin* (1998) is "Loyalty is bought, betrayal is a way of life."

About the Actor:

In an interview regarding working with Robert De Niro on *Ronin* (1998), Jean Reno said that Robert De Niro is a fantastic actor.

"Oh, man. I can't fucking believe this. Another basement. Another elevator. How can the same shit happen to the same guy twice?"

Bruce Willis as Lt. John McClane – ***Die Hard 2 Die Harder (1990)***

Setting:

McClane talks to himself after arguing with those in the control tower and climbing out of the top of the elevator to go solo in finding out what is going on at the airport. This is right before he meets the janitor, Marvin. A little later, crawling through a crawl space, he hears gunfire and continues to talk to himself, "Damn it. I hate it when I'm right."

Movie Trivia:

Tag lines for *Die Hard 2 Die Harder* (1990) include: "They say lighting never strikes twice … They were wrong." and "John McClane is back in the wrong place at the wrong time."

About the Actor:

Bruce Willis debuted as David Addison in *Moonlighting* on March 3, 1985.

"**Brad Wesley picked me. And when he did, he fucked up. I'm only good at one thing, Doc. I never lose.**"

Patrick Swayze as Dalton **– Road House (1989)**

Setting:

Dalton tells Doc Elizabeth Clay (Kelly Lynch) why he is the one who must stand up to Brad Wesley (Ben Gazzara).

Movie Trivia:

Ben Gazzara was nominated for a 1990 Razzie Award for Worst Supporting Actor for his role as Brad Wesley in *Road House* (1989).

About the Actor:

Patrick Swayze trained with Benny "The Jet" Urquidez, a Kickboxing Pro who never lost a professional match, for the fight scenes in *Road House* (1989).

"Nailed them both."

Danny Glover as Sergeant Roger Murtaugh – **Lethal Weapon 2 (1989)**

Setting:

Murtaugh comments to himself after using a nail gun to dispatch two would-be-killers that broke into his home.

Movie Trivia:

Mickey McGee, the Carpenter who was using the nail gun to fix Murtaugh's home, was played by Jack McGee.

About the Actor:

Danny Glover played Dr. Pratt's father, Charlie Pratt, Sr., in four episodes of the hit television series *ER* (2005).

"Make sure you spell my name right."

Joe Lewis as Jonathan Cross (Jaguar) – ***Jaguar Lives! (1979)***

Setting:

The reply to General Villanova (Donald Pleasence) when he tells Cross about a man he had shot, "He's buried here, beneath the floor. You shall have the space next to him, with a plaque of course."

Movie Trivia:

Jaguar Lives! (1979) was the first starring role for Karate Champion Joe Lewis. The movie also featured Christopher Lee, Donald Pleasence, Barbara Bach, Woody Strode, Anthony De Longis, and John Huston.

About the Actor:

Joe Lewis was extremely helpful when author Alain Burrese asked for help with an article he was working on for *Black Belt* magazine.

"Well, I've been knocked down, blown up, lied to, shit on, shot at. I'm not a virgin except in my heart. Nothing much surprises me anymore except what people do to each other. I'm a licensed pilot. I've lectured on economics at Yale. And I can memorize the front page of The New York Times in five minutes and repeat it back to you in five weeks. I was national Golden Gloves champion three years in a row, and I'm fluent in four languages, and … don't interrupt me, I'm not through … Yeah, I lie a lot."

Burt Reynolds as Nick 'Mex' Escalante – **Heat (1986)**

Setting:

Escalante tells Cyrus Kinnick (Peter MacNicol) his qualifications when Kinnick interviews him regarding a bodyguard job while Kinnick gambles.

Movie Trivia:

William Goldman wrote the novel and the screenplay for *Heat* (1986).

About the Actor:

The official Burt Reynolds website is www.burtreynolds.com.

"Chico, since when did anybody ever accuse me of being sane?"

Steven Seagal as John Hatcher – **Marked For Death (1990)**

Setting:

Hatcher's reply to his partner Chico's (Richard Delmonte) questions, "What are you? Are you crazy?" The two DEA agents are about to go into a meeting where they are supposed to be undercover, but Chico is sure they have been made.

Movie Trivia:

Hector, the criminal Hatcher and Chico chase, beat up, and lock in the trunk of the car at the beginning of *Marked For Death* (1990), is played by Danny Trejo, who has been in numerous television and movie roles, including *Heat* (1995) with Al Pacino and Robert De Niro and the title role in *Machete* (2010).

About the Actor:

Steven Seagal plays bad guy Torrez in *Machete* (2010) starring Danny Trejo.

"Sniper."

Jean-Claude Van Damme as Alain Moreau – **Maximum Risk (1989)**

Setting:

Alain Moreau's simple one word answer when Alex Minetti (Natasha Henstridge) asks, "What'd you do in the war?" as they look through things in Moreau's brother's apartment.

Movie Trivia:

Maximum Risk (1989) was directed by Hong Kong director Ringo Lam.

About the Actor:

Jean-Claude Van Damme played characters named Alain in *Maximum Risk* (1996) and *Legionnaire* (1998).

"In combat, you face the enemy without doubt, without pity or remorse. To survive, you must learn to fear nothing at all."

Sho Kosugi as Ozunu – **Ninja Assassin (2009)**

Setting:

Ozunu gives a speech to the young Raizo (Yoon Sungwoong) after a fight in the training grounds that left Raizo's brother lying on the ground. As training continues, so do Ozunu's lessons, "Pain breeds weakness. Remember, suffering exists only because weakness exists. You must hate all weakness. Hate it in others, but most of all, hate it in yourself." These lessons come with a lot of pain for the young Raizo, but they also make him the hero he becomes.

Movie Trivia:

Ninja Assassin (2009) was directed by James McTeigue. He also directed *V for Vendetta* (2005).

About the Actor:

Sho Kosugi was known for many ninja movies in the 1980s, including: *Enter the Ninja* (1981), *Revenge of the Ninja* (1983), *Ninja III: The Domination* (1984), and *Nine Deaths of the Ninja* (1985).

"You're a daisy if you do."

Val Kilmer as Doc Holliday – **Tombstone (1993)**

Setting:

Holliday's reply near the end of the shootout at the O.K. Corral, when his guns are empty and the man he is facing says, "I got you now, you son-of-a-bitch."

Movie Trivia:

It's reported that Doc Holliday actually did say, "You're a daisy if you do," to a Cowboy who confronted him at point blank range near the end of a gun battle.

About the Actor:

Val Kilmer's film debut was in the 1984 spoof *Top Secret!* (1984), where he starred as blond rock idol Nick Rivers.

"Hate Him back. It works for me."

Mel Gibson as Sergeant Martin Riggs – **Lethal Weapon (1987)**

Setting:

Riggs' reply to Roger Murtaugh's (Danny Glover) comment, "God hates me, that's what it is."

Movie Trivia:

The first *Lethal Weapon* (1987), along with *Die Hard* (1988), is credited with setting new standards for urban action films.

About the Actor:

Mel Gibson moved to Australia with his parents when he was 12 years old.

"Travis Brickley doesn't dance."

Eric Roberts as Alexander Grady – **Best of the Best 2 (1993)**

Setting:

Alex Grady and Tommy Lee (Phillip Rhee) confront colosseum manager Weldon (Wayne Newton), looking for their friend Travis Brickley (Christopher Penn), who fought there earlier that night.

Movie Trivia:

Max Storm and John Allen Nelson are credited as writers for *Best of the Best 2* (1993). Max Storm was also credited with writing additional dialog for the original *Best of the Best* (1989). John Allen Nelson and Max Storm also worked together writing the screenplay for *American Yakuza* (1993).

About the Actor:

Eric Roberts was nominated for an Oscar for Best Actor in a Supporting Role for his performance as Buck in *Runaway Train* (1985).

"All right. Who else wants some?"

Steven Seagal as Nico Toscani – **Above the Law (1988)**

Setting:

Toscani takes out three "tough guys" in a bar while looking for his cousin Lucy (Michelle Hoard). He then addresses the rest of the bar.

Movie Trivia:

Pam Grier, star of the 1970s movies such as *Coffy* (1973) and *Foxy Brown* (1974), and the Quentin Tarantino hit *Jackie Brown* (1997), played Nico's partner Delores 'Jacks' Jackson.

About the Actor:

Steven Seagal co-wrote and co-produced *Above the Law* (1988), his film debut.

"I hate a son-of-a-bitch that gets up noisy and full of himself."

Kris Kristofferson as Billy the Kid – **Pat Garrett and Billy the Kid (1973)**

Setting:

Billy and others are woken up by one of the crew.

Movie Trivia:

Bob Dylan made his movie debut in *Pat Garrett and Billy the Kid* (1973) as Alias. He also composed the music and sang the soundtrack.

About the Actor:

Kristoffer Dristian Kristofferson was born June 22, 1936, in Brownsville, Texas.

"Captain, Danny and I came up together, 15 years on the fucking street. Whoever killed him's going to pay. I'm going to finish it."

Danny Glover as Lieutenant Mike Harrigan – ***Predator 2 (1990)***

Setting:

Lt. Harrigan makes this comment about the murder of Danny Archuleta (Ruben Blades) to Captain B. Pilgrim (Kent McCord) just after Captain Phil Heinemann (Robert Davi) tells him to stay out of it and let Peter Keyes (Gary Busey) and the feds handle it, and right before Harrigan chases Keyes downstairs, jacks him up against the wall and tells him, "Listen, shithead. I don't give a fuck who you really are or what you want with this asshole. Because now it's personal, and he's a dead man." When Keyes tells him he does not know what he's dealing with, Harrigan replies, "You don't know what you're dealing with. And I'm warning you, stay the fuck out of my way!"

Movie Trivia:

Danny Glover and Gary Busey appeared together three years earlier in *Lethal Weapon* (1987), the same year *Predator* (1987) with Arnold Schwarzenegger was released.

About the Actor:

While a teenager, Danny Glover developed epilepsy, which he learned to control by a form of self-hypnosis. The epileptic seizures stopped after the age of 35.

"When I get back, I'm going to kill you."

Kurt Russell as Snake Plissken – **Escape From New York (1981)**

Setting:

Plissken tells Hauk (Lee Van Cleef) what he's going to do when he gets back after Hauk has tiny explosives put in Plissken's neck and tells him they'll burn out the charges if he makes it back in time with the President, and if he doesn't make it in time, "No more Snake Plissken."

Movie Trivia:

Escape From New York (1981) was written and directed by John Carpenter. Nick Castle was the co-writer.

About the Actor:

Kurt Russell is good friends with director John Carpenter, and *Escape From New York* (1981) is one of five films in which the two have collaborated.

"I'll start trembling in a minute."

Bruce Willis as Joe Hallenbeck – **The Last Boy Scout (1991)**

Setting:

When Milo (Taylor Negron) wants a formal introduction after Hallenbeck killed Chet (Kim Coates), Hallenbeck blows him off and says, "You're the bad guy, right?" Milo answers, "I am the bad guy." Hallenbeck then says, "And I'm supposed to be trembling with fear, something like that?" Milo says, "Something like that." This quote is Hallenbeck's reply.

Movie Trivia:

Hallenbeck's tan car is a 1971 Buick "Boat Tail" Riviera.

About the Actor:

Bruce Willis visited Iraq as part of the USO tour in 2003. He sang to the troops with his band, The Accelerators.

"Which one of those did you just piss in?"

Steven Seagal as Lt. Jack Cole – ***The Glimmer Man (1996)***

Setting:

Capt. Harris (Ryan Cutrona) demands Cole's ID and Badge while in the bathroom after Cole passed the polygraph. Cole says the above and tosses his badge in the urinal.

Movie Trivia:

The Glimmer Man (1996) was a Seagal/Nasso Production.

About the Actor:

Steven Seagal and Julius R. Nasso owned Seagal/Nasso Productions from 1994-2000.

"What's up, Doc?"

Clive Owen as Smith – **Shoot 'Em Up (2007)**

Setting:

Smith takes a bite out of a carrot before interrupting Hertz (Paul Giamatti), who was trying to force Donna Quintano (Monica Bellucci) to tell him where the baby is. When Hertz turns his gun toward Smith and calls him a "wascally wabbit, but not wascally enough." Smith replies, "That's a six-shooter. I just counted six shots. You've blown your load."

Movie Trivia:

Shoot 'Em Up (2007) is obviously not an "Oscar" type movie, but both Clive Owen and Paul Giamatti have been nominated for Oscars for other films: Owen for Best Performance by an Actor in a Supporting Role for *Closer* (2004), and Giamatti for Best Performance by an Actor in a Supporting Role for *Cinderella Man* (2005).

About the Actor:

Clive Owen won a Golden Globe for Best Performance by an Actor in a Supporting Role in a Motion Picture for his role in *Closer* (2004).

"Yeah, yeah, it's not my blood."

Bruce Willis as John McClane – **Die Hard With a Vengeance (1995)**

Setting:

McClane comes out of the elevator in the federal building spattered with blood from the bad guys he just killed. He meets Zeus Carver (Samuel L. Jackson) in the basement who asks him, "You all right?"

Movie Trivia:

Samuel L. Jackson was allowed to handle a real gold bar to assist him in making it look real when he was carrying the fake movie gold bar in the film.

About the Actor:

Bruce Willis is the eldest of four children. His siblings included his sister Florence, and brothers David and Robert.

"Just remember what old Jack Burton does when the earth quakes, and the poison arrows fall from the sky, and the pillars of Heaven shake. Yeah, Jack Burton just looks that big ol' storm right square in the eye and he says, 'Give me your best shot, pal. I can take it.'"

Kurt Russell as Jack Burton – ***Big Trouble in Little China (1986)***

Setting:

Final line said by Burton on his CB radio.

Movie Trivia:

The song "Big Trouble in Little China" playing when the credits roll was written by John Carpenter and performed by The Coupe de Villes.

About the Actor:

Kurt Russell told John Carpenter during the commentary of *Big Trouble in Little China* (1986) that *Escape From New York* (1981) was the best experience from a film he ever had. He said doing the film was as much fun as seeing it.

To Be Continued...

INDEX

MOVIES

ACTORS

ABOUT THE AUTHOR

Alain Burrese is the author of *Hard-Won Wisdom From The School Of Hard Knocks*, eight instructional DVDs on martial arts and self-defense, a thriller titled *Lost Conscience*, and the *Tough Guy Wisdom* series. He is currently working on additional titles to the *Tough Guy Wisdom* series, another novel, additional instructional DVDs, and several other projects. Alain's background includes serving as a paratrooper with the 82nd Airborne Division, a sniper instructor for the 2nd Infantry Division, living and training in Japan and South Korea where he earned a 4th degree black belt in the self-defense art of Hapkido, teaching, bodyguarding, speaking, mediating, practicing law, security, and various other positions throughout the years. He currently lives in Montana with his wife and daughter, and when not with them, he spends his time writing, teaching, speaking, and helping others resolve conflict. That, and of course, watching tough guy movies.

TOUGH GUY WISDOM SERIES

Tough Guy Wisdom II: Return of the Tough Guy
Tough Guy Wisdom III: Revenge of the Tough Guy

Future Volumes:

Tough Guy Wisdom: John Wayne vol. 1
Tough Guy Wisdom: John Wayne vol. 2
Tough Guy Wisdom: Clint Eastwood
Tough Guy Wisdom: Charles Bronson
Tough Guy Wisdom: Chuck Norris
Tough Guy Wisdom: Sylvester Stallone
Tough Guy Wisdom: Arnold Schwarzenegger
Tough Guy Wisdom: Rise of the Super Heroes
Tough Guy Wisdom IV
Tough Guy Wisdom V
Tough Guy Wisdom VI
Tough Guy Wisdom VII…

www.ingramcontent.com/pod-product-compliance
Lightning Source LLC
Chambersburg PA
CBHW071535040426
42452CB00008B/1020